Continental Shelf

FRED D'AGUIAR was born in London in 1960 to Guyanese parents and grew up in Guyana, returning to England when he was a teenager. He trained as a psychiatric nurse before reading African and Caribbean Studies at the University of Kent, Canterbury. His previous collections of poetry are *Mama Dot* (1985), *Airy Hall* (1989; winner of the Guyana Poetry Prize), *British Subjects* (1993) and *Bill of Rights* (1998; shortlisted for the T.S. Eliot Prize), all published by Chatto. His *An English Sampler: New and Selected Poems* appeared in 2001. Fred D'Aguiar is also the author of four novels, the first of which, *The Longest Memory* (Pantheon, 1994), won both the David Higham Prize for Fiction and the Whitbread First Novel Award. His plays include *High Life* (1987) and *A Jamaican Airman Foresees His Death* (1991), which was performed at the Royal Court Theatre, London. Fred D'Aguiar was Judith E. Wilson Fellow at Cambridge University from 1989-90 and has taught in the United States since 1992. He is currently Professor of English and Gloria D. Smith Professor of Africana Studies at Virginia Tech State University.

FRED D'AGUIAR

Continental Shelf

CARCANET

First published in Great Britain in 2009 by
Carcanet Press Limited
Alliance House
Cross Street
Manchester M2 7AQ

A CIP catalogue record for this book is available from the British Library
ISBN 978 1 84777 043 1

The publisher acknowledges financial assistance from Arts Council England

Typeset by XL Publishing Services, Tiverton
Printed and bound in England by SRP Ltd, Exeter

For Wilson Harris

Acknowledgements

My thanks to the editors of the following magazines in which some poems appeared: *Agni, Edinburgh Review, Exact Change Yearbook*, the *Caribbean Review of Books*, the *Caribbean Writer, New Writing*, the *New Yorker, Massachusetts Review, PN Review, Poetry London, Poetry Review, Poetry* and the *Times Literary Supplement*.

Extracts from 'Elegies' were broadcast or published in the following places: Part One of the poem was commissioned by Julian May for *Last Words* on BBC Radio 4, and a version with additional material was subsequently broadcast on *The Ticket* on the BBC World Service. A short version of Part Two was commissioned by Kevin Dawson for *The Word* on the BBC World Service. Other sections of the poem were published in *Callaloo* (US), *Poetry Review* (UK), *Atlas* (India), the *Guardian* online and at www.othervoices.org (edited by Roger Humes); and broadcast on ABC Radio, Perth, Australia.

I thank Michael Schmidt for his generous embrace of this collection, Stephen Procter for his organisation, and amplified thanks to Judith Willson who knows all about the devil in the details. Geoff Hardy, as a student teacher of English at my secondary school, helped me to find the key – from a bunch of keys – to a door I lingered outside for some time, that led to the land of poetry as an art and craft and, with his partner Peter Roscoe, we've sustained a creative friendship which continues to inspire my poetry and life. I thank the poet and producer Julian May for his gifted radio production of parts of the 'Elegies' poem. A similar shout of gratitude goes to Kevin Dawson for his radio artistry with parts of 'Elegies'. So much of the great art of Frank Bowling suited this collection but I could only pick one painting.

Contents

Local Colour

Continental Shelf

Local Colour

Bring Back, Bring Back

Bring back morning ice in enamel buckets
Fetched two at a time for balance from standpipes
Set at village squares, pipes shared by villages
Too numerous to name properly and too few to do
Anything but name for qualities shown by folk
Interviewed by administrators in hard hats on
Horseback way before Model-T and the Wrights'
First flight, when my grandparents, mere tadpoles,
Swished around in their parents as nothing more
Than wishes thought up in fields while minding
Indolent cows, sheep or goats or while poised
Over washing on a ribbed scrubbing board;
Bring them back as you would sprinters to a start line
After a false start where one bolts and the rest follow.

A Clean Slate

for Grace Theriault-Mayfield

Each morning I worked up spit
Aimed at my slate and wiped
Shirt-tail from corner to corner

Each day was a clean start
Born again and born *big-so*
As grownups loved to say

The day before disappeared
Somewhere between
My saliva and Terylene shirt

The new day promised
Something hitherto not
Seen or guessed about

A cobweb not there
The previous twenty-four hours
That overnight dew reveals

'A' for aubergine
Known to us as *balanjay*
'B' for bat for playing cricket

Until I filled the slate
With slant text my left hand
Told my right-side brain was new

Coins on the sea pressed by light
This morning sky wiped of stars
Chalk off my shirt climbing sun

The Return

for Ruby and Victor Ramraj

Whether Titta stands for sister or no
No more icepick and its flint on the blockhead of ice

Whether Mama Dot stands for Grandma Dorothy or no
No more right hand cutlass swings at the left hand's juice and jelly

Whether Cooperative Republic village number 162 stands for Airy
                                                                Hall or no
No more full-frontal kiss of cars on the pronounced curves of the
                                                                S-road
That's the only road into town

Whether guinep or stinking-toe or sour-sop or jamoon stand for
                                                                fruits or no
No more sprints from the house at the first smell of rain in nothing
                                                        but our peeled skin

Whether to lime is to hang and to gaff or labrish is to shoot the
                                                                breeze or no
No more shielding the wick of the oil lamp as I duck under the
                                                                top half
While I toe open the bottom half of the back door's half-doors

Whether Backdam stands for Koker or no
No more going Dutch for a day trip to Kyk-Over-Al
Where the Essequibo spreads like a sea
Where the Mazaruni and the Cuyuni part mineral company

Whether Kaieteur falls for a record 741-foot single drop or no
No more eye-turn head-spin shuffle of up and down
So that the falls rise and the forest canopy bows to the floor

Whether Guyana is Kanaima or no
Whether I-an-I stands for you and me or no

At Sea

All night I rock, twist and turn.
I wish it was my baby who was on my mind.

Blame that two-week crossing of the Atlantic
By boat back in '62, from England to Guyana,

When I learned to rock and roll effortlessly,
And the world, the whole liquid enterprise of it,

Seemed to be going someplace, leaving me
Behind or in the middle of nowhere,

At a point that kept the horizon exactly
In the distance and brought dolphins to the side

Then sent them off, and saw whales dipping
And rising together, relocating an archipelago

Of sudden springs that died as suddenly
As begun, as they headed away, always away

From me, dancing in reluctant sways, swivels
And spins on the spot, in a world of flux.

Reap

Combine harvester in '68 big as the house
Twenty children deep ironed the rice fields
Flat as day-old stubble on my uncle's chin,

Filled the basement with paddy bags,
Built a child's palace of hay and sun
Kept simmering in caves burrowed
By hands too small to do more than idle.

Steady rain of engine noise for sleeping,
Fumes for stewing in that spin my head
Back whenever I catch a whiff from a car.

I carry the behemoth miniaturised in me,
Portable as history and potable as basil,
Ready for my skull's low flame that needs
Just a touch, a pinch to water mouth and eyes.

Calypso

I stuttered in Georgetown,
Guyana, in 1966, and was so ashamed
I did not speak even when spoken to,

Until I heard one song that ran,
'I don't know, I don't know,' a long
'o' in that second 'know' converted

doubt to wonder itself, and continued,
'Why they got people bad-minded so,'
repeating the couplet erased all doubt,

that independence year of overproof
rum and absolutes. The singer groaned
how his efforts only invited envy,

how ingrained failure made a stranger
of success, then he launched this boast:
'I got the rhythm,' three times no less,

adding his own made-up word – what a cheek –
'tan-tantilism.' That extra tan stretched,
creolised, ironed smooth my creased tongue.

Was I alone in the capital in not joining
the country's club of bad minds ranged
against singer and song after it stuck

all year in the charts? Everything about
1966, six feet below sea-level,
drained from me, everything except

that little strain lodged in my skull
and always budding on my tongue.
It tea-teases, tau-taunts, tan-tantalises.

Railway

Long before you see train
The tracks sing and tremble,
Long before you know direction
Train come from, a hum
Announces it soon arrive.
So we tend to drop on all fours
Even before we look left or right.
We skip the sleepers or walk
Along by balancing on a rail.
We talk about the capital
Where the train ends its run
From the interior laden with
The outsized trunks of felled
Trees and open-topped cars of bauxite.
We always hide from it unsure
What the train will do if we
Stand next to the tracks.
It flattens our nails into knives,
It obliterates any traffic
Caught by it at crossroads,
It whistles a battle cry,
Steam from the engine a mood
Not to mess with or else.
Rails without beginning or end,
Twinned hopes always at your back,
Always up front beckoning you on,
Double oxen, hoof stomp, temper
Tantrum, stampede, clatter
Matter, head splitter, hear us,
Stooped with an ear to the line –
greenheart, mora, baromalli,
purple heart, crabwood,
kabakalli, womara.

Tributary

The hand I dipped into glass
For a sip to grease my throat
Whose ballbearings turned on sand
That half-formed M in my palm
Lifted what it could to my lips
Losing what it could not contain
Thru imperfectly locked fingers
So that I almost kissed a tadpole
Stenciled it seemed to complete
M for Mahaicony River
Had I closed my eyes as I do
When I drink from this fridge
On the move I would have
Taken that tadpole in as one
Takes in someone or something
Bumped into by chance when
The mood is right and the feel
For water on the move caught
In a corner pool supports
Tadpoles and invites the thirsty
To lean in, lean down and sup
There, dip drink, dip kiss,
One tadpole to another, tail
Swapped for legs, legs bifurcated
As the tail they used to be.

H_2O

Empty buckets swing as
we traipse to the standpipe
a quarter of a mile away,
sun-up and sun-down,
for drinking and cooking
water stored in ringed barrels
kept on wood plinths under
steps that lead to the kitchen
where things happen to water,
sizzles and gurgles,
splutters and perfumed steam
culminated in a spanking
meal of steady depletion;

our walk to the standpipe
full of talk and languor,
our return laden with two
buckets whose Richter
charts our crawl
home trying not to spill
one heavenly drop,
eyes locked on the path
for the next step to land
even and send small ripples
from surface-centre
to bucket-edge and back,
if lucky, nothing over the side.

Someone tall stationed at
barrels lifts our buckets,
tips contents into drums,
that fill from a brassy sound
of flustered metal to muffled
contentment of water
breaking the fall of water,
and us back on the trail,
headed for the standpipe,
our aluminum buckets wanting,
the sound of water pouring,
poured, crowds our heads,
promises full barrels soon, soon.

Matriarch

In the dry season
she sprinkles water
in the yard to keep the dust
down, dust that otherwise
flies through slatted windows.
Cool takes shape as shadows
locked in a house on stilts.
Underneath a dog pants in sleep
paws flicked in a chase.
Her headache soothes, forehead
wrapped in Limocol-soaked linen.
Children tiptoe around the house,
speak in water trickles.
Laughter explodes behind
sealed lips and eyes
whitened wide. If there is
mercy here it is accidental
and lives in the flea's
escape from two thumbnails
squashed together shooting
said flea between floorboards.
By late afternoon the yard
dries and spins a crop
of whirlwinds house high.

Something Imagined

Not just rain but slant, dust-raising pebbles,
not those globules but their flash flood
sweeping donkey and cart away, not their loss
but how we find each still harnessed to each buried
deep in mud and grime; not only debris with a name
whistled and a stick flicked at a flank and a cart-pace,
but all the times we look for rain and nothing but light falls
from the unblinking sun; not that hot brand but its partner
moon; not the moon but our man in it and the cheese
of it and any river wound-up by all three; not any river
but the Mahaicony's current that charges the eel and shines
fluorescent when ground yields as if my next step falls
on air conveying pollen, metals, and peeled skin; not that air
but the bullfrog who needs it all to bellow; not that roar;
my mother's wet hair tied in a towel and bunched on her skull;
not her skull but the image of her as nothing but bones;
not her bones, nor her dust, but a parchment's need for water
to find that donkey and cart once more and ride standing;
name and a whistle and stick measuring the journey home.

Tamarind Season

Tamarinds hide all summer for us to find them,
Gnarled fists closed around our hopes,
Keepsakes for mouths starved of sour things,
Seeded conviction against army ants,
We pick them like puff cotton bolls
With the moon in them, except they keep
What's ours, what can't be gifted
Even if desired to give, even if wanted,
The push and pull, nods and headshake
Passed hand to mouth, thick with deceit,
The tamarinds, dry by the time we approach,
Rattle their tails and stop us dead in our tracks.
Outside, we act like men, inside, we're boys
Who mistake the snake's rattle for one of our toys.

Playing House

We collected brown branches
Fallen from coconut palms
Propped them against a tree
For a centre post in a tent

You brought a pinch of salt
I grabbed two handfuls of rice
You found a match I found a tin pot
We struck up flames between stones

Half-filled the pot with water
Brought it to the boil
Added the salt and I licked
Grains stuck to your palm

Dumped in the rice after we
Picked it clean of stalks
Watched the pot though
We knew all about watched pots

And for plates we used dasheen
Leaves and for spoons our
Fingers and we talked with
Our mouths full about children

How many we would have
And the ratio of boys to girls
You wanted more girls
I preferred more boys

And that would have been that
Were it not for the tiredness
After a meal that necessitated
Sleep in our little tent of coconut

Branches and the two of us
Curled up together as we
Imagined we would be
When we grew big and began

All this building of a house
And cooking and planning
For children in earnest
But for now we sleep

ROYGBIV

The shoemaker's wife ran preschool
With a fist made not so much of iron
But wire bristles on a wooden brush.

She made us recite and learn by rote.
Our trick was to mouth words, sound
As if we knew what we would one day

Come to know, what would dawn
On us as sure as a centipede knows
What to do with its myriad legs.

She made us settle our feet on the mud
Floor of her daub and wattle hut and she
Wielded a cane cut from wood that bit

Into the palm of the hand and left a burn
That resonated up the arm for an age
After its smart swing and crisp contact.

Worst of all was the shoe cupboard
Where the old man stored his wire
Brushes: a cold, dark, narrow place,

Replete with brushes hung on nails
Covering every square inch and said
To come alive when a child was locked

In with them so that they scrubbed
Flesh off that child's bones. She said
We would end up there if we did not

Concentrate, so we stilled our feet
And spoke the words in the right order
For colours in a rainbow until the very

Thing took her place in front of us
Arranged in cuneiform, polished,
Brandishing a window to climb out.

Caribbean

Sunlight curled from wood
Planed by a carpenter
Speckled with a shaved light
Cut-wood rose smell

Breeze dank with seaweed
Tossed by currents rolled in sand
By waves and left to sun
Battered and deep-fried

Palm branches ribbed with light
Segmented shadows breathing
Swimming at crawl-pace across
Ground that's a clock-face

Empty belly feeds on conch
Shell and grumbles most
Afternoons with thunder
Lightning and downpours

Let the galvanised zinc
Of the sea write on sand
Erase what it writes and pull
Away fast from this place

For some other republic
Peddling sunshine and steel
Pan and flora so brightly lit
You need shades to look

For your stomach to quiet
Its rebel music and siesta
Shoes under your head
Hat over your eyes

Bullroarer

Heads you win, tails you lose, I said
Or you said, as we gambled over who
Should go first once the thing was made.
You flipped the quarter and I picked
Or my flip meant you picked, which
Way around only matters because that
Really happened and what really happened
Also got us started from scratch.

First we eat the ice sleeve on the stick
Little by little, you bite off and give to me,
I nibble a piece and feed it to you, until
We wear it down and expose the flat
Cylindrical wood to air and see how half
Is the colour of flavoured icicle and half
Our fingerprints, thumb on one side
Index finger on the other.

Next I direct a razorblade down
The middle of the stick and split
Less than a half-inch slit at the dry end.
You bite a three-foot piece of thread
From a spool with a needle stuck in it
And I caution you against swallowing
That needle by accident and we laugh
At the horror of such a thing ever.

Any colour thread completes the trick.
Wind some around the opening
Into a knot and the contraption is ready.
(Since my call won or you called wrong
I get to go first and offer it to you
But you insist that I won fair and square.)
For what happens when I swing the thread
Attached to the lolly-stick, just above

My head, us patient for several turns,
The stick twisting, twisting till the wood sings,
Always happens as long as I labour, with only
A pause in its song when the coil changes
Direction for more unspooled music:
A hummingbird stickling in mid-air;
A dreadlocked nest of bees in a swirl;
Our geared-up, head over heels pitch.

The Barber-Green

As if licked with a coat of fresh paint
from a new season in a creeping forest knitted close
bright against the background of red sand road
bigger than a dump truck and matching in bulk
any grumbling combine harvester anyday
adrift in its inches-crawl and feed
on pot-holes and sand and stones
followed by a crew tied to it or so
they seemed the way they kept near
yet maintained a healthy out-of-swipe's-way
distance from it
                           made us reach for stones
fill our pockets and load both hands
and pelt the thing when it drew near
the house believing it could turn off
the road and bulldoze our house
garden and guinep tree then keep going
deep into the coconut grove
inching its way over all we knew
for what we did not know

this new smooth black bitumen
its fragrance of sweat and goodness
how a marble rolled on it kept going
propelled by tarmac and cars
careened off bends in the road
as the only means of stopping
unless one met another car head on
how the donkey with new shoes
lost its footing and simply sat
in the road attempting with pursed lips
to graze on crushed stones mixed with tar

Caiman

Bridge over trench
log in the right place
muddy and leaf-ridden
bark ruddy with weather
beating it like clothes
on a stone riverbank
threshold invites my foot
to step as into a shoe
found with my outstretched
toes clenched and then spread
grasping under bed frame

but my weight behind that foot
startles life into that bridge
which wriggles from side
to side in rapid tail twists
fast head sweeps
tail and head sprouted
on that log and all this
in that second of touch
with the ball of my foot and
the tips of my toes
before my weight settles down

all that thrown into instant
reverse so that I leap off that log
cycle in air and shout
involuntarily throwing
my arms out for balance
in a mad scramble from that trench
dry for the most part
catching sight of a wide mouth
and long tail taken for a bridge
caiman unlucky to miss me
miss lunch by inches

Snake and Ladder

The flat side of a cutlass
Slaps a cobra on the head
Grab that cobra by the tail
Chop off that cobra's head

An untrained hand and eye
Might swipe the poised head
Only to send that head flying
Straight into the body where

The fangs latch on and milky
Venom shoots though snake
Is separated head from body
So the first move is a slap

The merest tap by that cutlass
Flick the blade-wielding wrist

After Birth

I hold out my arms
posture begging for alms
and into my hands up to my elbows falls
lamb attached to cord strung between
mother and offspring complete
with ghoulish stuff for washing off
later with soap under
running water and a smile
no amount of reprimands could
wipe off my face
that lamb kicked away
from me and bounced around
hardly standing still for its mother's
lick and spit clean
lamb butting udder for milk to come
down quick-quick
flies circling the afterbirth
already as flies must
and me ready to taste it
as a mother might inhale
with her mouth clamped
over her child's blocked nose

Ledge

When my aunt begged me not to move
She stood in the yard and looked up
Two floors at me poised on the window
Ledge my little legs dangling over
The edge and my small hands braced
On the six-inch-wide wood whose paint
Rain washed and sun bleached away.

When she shouted for help I jumped
With fright and held on tight and chipped
Paint and saw how she disappeared
Under me so that I almost dropped off
My perch to catch up with her. How I
Got out there, an open window, a chair
Next to it perhaps, is anybody's guess.

It was the terrible twos and I was months
Early but firmly ensconced in it. Whoever
Was designated to watch me only had to
Turn from me for one second to lose me
To the vista of an open window with its
Portion of sky and channel for birdsong
And funnel of cool sea breeze and a drop

To the ground that meant nothing to me
Back then only that if I relaxed my grip
I could fall into the arms and upturned
Face of my favourite aunt not far below.
Between her scream and everyone and
Everything brought to a standstill – axe
On wood, enamel pots and pans, broom

Across floor, bucket dipped in water
Drum, pigs squabbling in a sty, donkey
Cut off mid-bray, dog bark stifled – my
Aunt dashed from me, around the house,
Climbed the stairs at least three at a time,
Cut through the bottom half of the half
Doors, crossed the room, and grabbed me.

Pan

for this story a verandah
at the top of eighteen steps
each with a gap underneath
that charts the climb up

if not for the banister I hold
for dear life I might not
make that ascent just
because of the ladder

made of air hoisted over
the yard and above the paling
fence around yard and guinep
tree a fixture of every yard

until air builds on air
in my head and makes it swim
so I hold on white-knuckled
barely able to trust one

foot put before another
till steps run out for boards
with no gaps dust cannot
fill or a rug or lamp-stand

the verandah closed in
all sides but the end down
those stairs and walled
chest high so I look

over and my head stays
clear with my body
braced against all that
timber lashed together

for safe keep of children
by the time the story begins
I lean on a post
shut my eyes and float

down that ladder of air
to the top of the guinep
tree and then the tip
of palings for a soft

landing on grass worn
brown by our heels
or else way up till I
drop off this world

and have to be borne
away by an adult
to my mattress
kingdom in the stars

S-Joe

Walked the way of the road
Leading into Airy Hall
With a twist and a turn
Hither and thither in line
With plates spun by a hand
None can see but many think
Must operate rods on which
Those plates balance and shimmer
As S-Joe shimmies a few feet
Stops on a sweet spot
Reverses for almost as many
Steps and then rolls forward
Getting nowhere fast
Folk said or with all the time
Afforded those spinning
Plates tilted twice
For S-Joe in keeping
With two bends in his name
And in the road whose
Open ends admit him
Whether he shuffles backwards
Or forwards eyes locked
On the melting always-ahead
Arms parked by his side
His knees lift and drop
With a hip and a hop
'S-Joe' we kids call 'S-Joe'
Following him from one
End of town to the next
Keeping just out of reach
In case he springs
From his trance
Again I call 'S-Joe'
For his response
As I would have it
On his behalf 'S-Joe'
Shadowing him
My road tied to his name

Dara Singh

Stepped off the continental shelf
Several mineral-rich feet below
Sea level into a capital of mud heads.
Above a canopy of monocot trees
Waved its approval with a flyover
From parakeets whose shifting rainbow
Reflected the ambition of a nation.
Dara Singh did not land so much as
Descend into Georgetown buoyed
By a crumbling seawall and made
Buoyant because Dara Singh was in
Town, to rahtid, yeah man, *the* Dara
Singh, prince of the square ring.
Schools let out early, shops closed
For extended lunch, buses ignored
Timetables for one staple that day:
The iron man from the mother country,
India, here to pacify all comers who dare
Step up to match grip and arm-locks
With him, India's answer to every
Question about native prowess be that
Physical or psychical or historical.
Never mind conquest and our status
As a newly independent colony,
Dara Singh here to set the record
Straight and any man worth his salt
Better be there to storify the day.
Singh stepped in the ring and emptied
It of all comers with a slap, kick, hard
Throw, elbow, glare and head butt.
Conquering lion, unvanquished
Tiger, Grizzly Bear among teddies.
1857 come again, bap! 1952 step
Forward, boom! 1966, pour the rum,
Slap the drum and wheel and turn,
Reverse the flow of the Amazon,
Shore up that seawall against history:
One wave after another lined up half
Way to the horizon with shoulders
Dipped for a charge we must absorb:
Dara Singh braced against our seawall.

Demerara Sugar

In neat sachets where each grain
Flows with crystal clarity in a slalom
Of Swiss blinds ready for my tongue

Sugar cut by hand-swinging cutlass
With half an eye kept on any snake
Wrapping its way around cane fields

Cane pressed for its last ounce of sap
Boiled down to molasses that is cane
Marrow if cane were bones broken

From fields for a bone feast
Demerara whose east coast raised me
From a mere stalk to stand straight

To stand tall no matter what current
Help me find your grain your flow
And Demerara sweeten me

So my art keeps your river's caveat
Your sense of cane fields bathed in sweat

Leaving

I left Mum, at the big house
Deep in country, for the capital.
The taxi kicked dust as I looked
Out the back windscreen into cloud,
My mother adrift and zeroing
Away from me. Copper strips
Buried in the taxi rear window,
Divided her into narrow segments
And allowed me to see her in parts,
One at a time, and feel her in portions,
Her entirety kindly apportioned
To fit my fifty-pound, sixth-year body.

For her head, long neck and round
Shoulders I cried without sound.
For her arms waving, I bawled.
For her torso and breasts I imagined
As mine for months after my birth,
I shouted her name, Mum, Mum.
For her waist that gyrated to calypso
As she carried me in her belly and
In her arms when the transistor played
Her favourite tune on the hit parade,
I begged her to keep me with her,
Between coughing fits and sleeving
My eyes so that I could make her out
Among cloud. And for her long legs
As she turned off the road to amble
Over log bridge, back to the house,
My head in my arms and my feet
Stamping the yielding rubber mat.

That was how I stored it for years.
In fact, she left me, not me her.
Mum twisted around in the cab.
I saw her head, neck and shoulders
Divided by those heat strips before
The car manufactured cloud with me
Occluded in it and beyond her reach.
I dashed after the hire, and my aunt
Swept me up and carried me kicking
And screaming across that log bridge
Back indoors, where I cried myself
Hoarse calling my mother and missed
Two meals and would have ignored a third
Were it not for black tea in an enamel cup
My aunt made for me, as I looked on,
Spooning (until she drew a smile from me)
As many sugars as my years, and chopping,
A veritable doorstop of a chunk of bread,
Fresh from the clay oven, and buttered so,
That the homespun clump of gold ran
Right off the slice and had to be caught
By my tongue stuck out without thinking.

Sabbatic

Drank methylated spirits and spat fire;
House so holey our missiles sailed
Right through. Lived alone but cursed,
Cried and threw furniture around
From midnight to predawn only to fall
Into a stupor and snore akin to a steam
Engine climbing a hill or a crate at a dock
Dropped from nine storeys to shatter
With a compact sound and a terrific
Explosion followed by utter quiet.
Her trip to the liquor store always
Grabbed us though she walked like
Any person on a mission and looked
Just like one, but it was Sabbatic
So we turned out to see her for sure,
After all her noise at night, us
Certain that something on her must
Break from hollering and throwing
Furniture about. But no, straw hat pulled
Low on her forehead she walked in light
That made her look nimble as this time
Of day made all things, living or dead.
Light that took away from the substance
Of bodies as if bones were rubber and flesh
Dropped like butter in a hot frying pan.
Adults said she was as thin as a rake and yes
She looked like a dressed-up rake, not in
Fineries, more like a scarecrow, though
Not raggedy as some scarecrows.
She walked on air on her outward
Journey and laden down home bound,
Clinking bottles measured her steps,
Eyes locked on the ground before her,
Ears corked to our pesky teasing:
Sabbatic, you forget to buy matches
To light the stove in your belly so you can
Spit fire! Sabbatic you need to buy new
Furniture so you can smash it up tonight!
Sabbatic, you house got more holes than
a strainer! Until an adult called us off,

Since she said nothing to us and never
Flinched at the stones we pelted.
Then one night we heard nothing
And could not see the trace of a lamp
She walked from room to room.
The adults whispered, gathered, gazed
At the house. An uncle crossed the empty
Lot separating our homes to shout her name.
Sabbatic! What happen, woman? Sabbatic!
Nothing. We hardly slept. We listened
To insects quarrel around lamps or in
Pitch blackness as if arguing with it.
They seemed to mimic Sabbatic.
First thing we followed the adults
To Sabbatic's house and waited in the yard
As they forced open her front door.
A single crow flew out and made
Even the adults cross themselves.
Then they rushed from the house
And chased us in front of them
And called the police. We heard bits
We pieced together since no
Adult would talk about Sabbatic
And the coroner stayed with the police
At the house a long time and left
With nothing but a steel canister.
According to the talk the adults
Found nothing in the house, no
Trace of Sabbatic, only a pile
Of ashes and no other mark of
A fire anywhere in the rooms.
All the bottles lay in neat stacks
Waiting for a drinker to weigh in
On them. The holes in the house
Gaped more than ever and never
Invited another missile from us,
Now nothing more than poor
People's holes no one looks at
Directly to save face and keep grace,
Holes for wind to howl through,
For rain to sail unabashedly.

The Shell Pond

What a day. No cloud in sight,
Breeze that could not divert a feather,
Sun with a roasting in store for all
Who dare venture out, man, even
Sunflowers want to find shade.
We watch the shell pond from
Doors, windows and verandahs
And rub we hands and wet we lips.
The pond full of sun self if that solid
Melt under he own steam and fall
Ba-daps, in a circle by the house,
But emerald and diamond studs
All over it and pleats for dressing,
A look like it contain everything
Under the sky, could take anything,
Including us, sent from the feet
Of adults, we sprint to the pond
Tearing off rags along the way:
Shirts pull over heads, trousers
Kick off, skirts, blouses, underwear
Only item we keep on only if you
Over ten, otherwise why bother?
Maye among us and we mindful
Of the younger ones as we dive
Surface and dip down again
Taking we face close to the shells
On the bottom like we grazing
Or something and following orders
Not to disturb mud and cloud water.

Who miss Maye first?
Who say Where Maye gone?
Somebody shout from balcony,
Jump fence, and dive straight
In with clothes on his back,
And come up clutching Maye
Who limp, he eye and mouth
Open, Maye, who nobody
Miss till now when he not
Answering to he name.
Count and pump he chest,

Blow air in he mouth.
The sun gone from he eye.

We all shouting he name
Maye, come back.
More air blow in he face
More fist pound he chest.
Who see where cloud
Come from? The shell
Pond take up the same
Cloud, we turn we back,
On sun and shell pond,
Just as we start to traipse
Indoors or hold up
Each other from collapse,
Just when the count,
Air in mouth and chest
Pound should stop
And let everything
Cover up with cloud,
Let the breeze pick up,
Let rain spiral down,
Let flood water come
And trap us indoors
For days of peeping
Through slatted windows,
Just then Maye cough up
Water, choke down air.
We fire plenty cheer
And run and carry
Him shoulder high
As the first drops
Raise dust and beat
Them back down, turn
Sand into mud and then
Streams finding pond,
Maye get back he shine.
What a day.

National Cycle Championship

We queued by the road
directly in front of the house,
waterbottles on strings ready
for Uncle who would sweep
into town at the front of the pack.
We posted a lookout in the guinep
tree and asked him every minute
if he caught any scrap of activity,
when he said not an atom
we looked at him quizzically.
Uncle got to turn up soon
after his mornings out before
dawn and alone with nothing
but owls, foxes, and his wheels
singing the day into fruition;
same routine at dusk as if
night could only fall to his tyres
eating up miles of country road.
We polished the spokes for him,
practised smiles in chrome rims,
dropped handle bars and frame
painted red and gold and green.
We turned it upsidedown and spun
wheels, listened and looked hard
as sprockets ticked and fussed
spic and span. He left a day early
for the capital and now at midday
we waited for him to pass the house
and confirm his standing as our
village champion sent to teach
the capital a thing or two about
bikes and drive and put us on
the map once and for all. We
were in a daze when the call
came from the topmost branch
of the guinep tree and it shook
as the lookout tumbled to join
us by the road and nearly broke
his limbs. We sprang around
while adults cajoled us to keep

off the road and watch for Uncle.
Of course we would watch for
Uncle and who would see him
first became the new contest.
One looked for his bike another
for his yellow and black jersey,
a third for the legs he rubbed
with coconut oil and knew by
touch as much as sight. This
was the Uncle who qualified
on a makeshift track in a clearing
by lapping his opponents even
after he fell at each bend.
Police on motorcycles, lights
flashing and horns blaring
signalled everyone off the road.
The lead riders hugged the corner
the bulk of the pack close behind
in a swoop that filled Airy Hall,
their heads down along the straight,
bikes thrown from side to side,
a mass of legs and arms, one
creature able to isolate joints
and propel along in a messy
tangle of shifts and shakes.
There was Uncle, as expected,
on our side of the road, tilted
for a bottle from one of us,
he winked at me, his face
plastered with a smile as broad
as this country that bred him.
The pack thinned to stragglers
and cars with spares and more police.
We danced and shouted, clapped,
slapped thighs, and shook heads.
We knew it would be two hours
before they came back for
the home run to the finish
line in the capital and we
kicked dirt not knowing
how one hundred and twenty
measly minutes could drag
feet so and loiter and hang,

nor why the sun so keen
to rob us of daylight would
today of all days just stick
in the sky directly overhead
and grip time in a headlock.
The lookout complained that
balancing on a swaying branch
forty feet in the air for two
hours was not the easiest
thing to do, he was allowed
down on condition that he
climb back at least fifteen
minutes before the expected
return. We ate grated coconut
held together with brown
sugar, cornsticks and drank
Mauby and sucked on crushed
ice doused with syrup. We skipped
rope, played hopscotch, all
in the front yard near the road.
Someone's *Boy, look at the time!*
jolted us, we dropped every
thing and scrambled for a ring
side place by the road;
the lookout clambered
back to the uppermost limb
able to support him and we
peered up the road and back
up at him for a sign and none
came and the sun kept
its crawl that was now a
treading on the spot where
the sky is deepest and farthest
from us, where crows circle
for hours on one wingbeat
and disappear if you stare
at them, melting into that
blue. He scrambled down
without a word of warning
and we know what that mean
for sure so we crane we neck
and lean in the road and the
police pass and wave us back

and then the pack swoop
round the corner and dig
into their peddles and sway
and we look for Uncle
sure to be up front matching
the best of them step by step.
We count the first line, then
two, three, four and somebody
call out if we miss he or what?
No one sure what going on
now he not in the pack either
and the stragglers pass and no
Uncle in sight and we asking
adults if they know some
thing we don't know since
Uncle nowhere to be seen,
and we see him blaze through
not two hours before in charge
at the front as he steered
the pack to the interior.
A truck pull up and we
see the mangled bicycle first
and we run from the side
of the truck to the back,
Uncle strains to sit up, the
skin scraped off his left leg,
his side and left arm, his face
all scrunched as he grips
the shoulders dipped either
side for him and they lift him
delicately from the truck and
carry him to the house.
We stand rooted to the spot
grappling with the notion
that the race gone to the capital
and Uncle here, with his warped
racer. Whoever start to clap
break our reverie and we
all join in so that before
Uncle reach the house
the solitary drip of applause
that start for him burgeons,
festoons this waterfall,
whistles and shouts of his name.

Subaltern

I missed my grandmother's funeral,
Missed too, Granddad's planting of a coconut
Grove to honour her memory, missed, in fact,
Her coming up as much as her going under,
If truth were told, since she lived more
Dead than when she breathed and walked
Boards I scrubbed with a scraper every Saturday
Morning in Airy Hall, an address we played with
Ad infinitum, *near Mahaicony, East Coast
Demerara, Guyana, South America, Earth*, her name
Uttered on more lips by people she birthed, washed,
Scolded, gave away or doused with a sponge all night
Through fever, shook awake from nightmares,
Accompanied in dreams of light that held sway
Over them like the hammock we christened,
Yellow Submarine, made from stitched
Paddy bags and slung between two basement rafters,
We all piled into and rocked and sang '*We all live…*'

I pictured her grave one thousand different ways,
Until I clapped eyes on it and forgot all but one
Way of looking when laid to rest: her headstone,
Fifty yards behind the house, among coconut trees
Whose dry fruit crash-land unannounced,
Beside my grandfather, their hands, so I fancy,
Clasped across the divide, tunnelled in sleep
Far from light, from naked sight, heads turned
Sideways, seeing each other in a death stare,
Plastered smile, darkness-governed, stillness
For life and us above her and him keeping
What we know of the two on our breaths now,
Always, as if they cared enough to reach up,
Touch our bare feet when we passed with our heads
In the air, mindful of unhinged, dry coconuts.
Solar System, Milky Way, Galaxy, Universe…

The Never-Never

Never our bodies lit by a lamp whose wick
Shoulders an oil snake for a flame
Licking soot onto the glass lamp
Casting a shadow diluted orange
As the slow burn of your kiss would have it
As my memory insists upon pitching it

And never the old cartwheel on one spot
Repeated until the eyes revolve in the head
And the earth-spin takes on a caterwauling
Laying the fine hairs in my inner ear flat
As I am laid out on my willing back
As my back flattens itself on the earth's map

Never the owl whose eye centres a storm
And the storm that mimics a star's fall
For breeze kills that oil lamp
Leaves one big shadow for a world
As I am there with you and both of us
As twins in that dark that fuses us

Never a book opened for anything
But reprimand and nothing but rules
In any book worth opening or so it seemed
Waist-high with things that gripped me
As a wave grips the sea and sea grips sand
As a current runs through the sky's open hand

Houses not Homes

Our dog, tethered under the house
on stilts, chewed through his lead, ran
next door to the slaughterhouse and drank
blood of the slaughtered multitudes.

Our dog lay sick for a week
howled, whimpered and died with a final
gasp. We buried him in the yard,
thanked him for watching
Mother's bicycle and our house.

We moved soon afterwards,
away from the railway line
and abattoir, for an apartment
in a house split down the middle
for two families. We climbed
rafters and battled the boys
next door and watched our
mother with her boyfriend
through cracks in the wall
where caulk rotted away.

My older brother pitted
against the eldest boy next door
fought until both fell
exhausted into a final hug.
Not to be confused with
the broken bottle incident
when my brother wrestled
a boy from the orphanage
who grabbed a bottle and cut
my brother's leg in a mark
we likened to Zorro's.

We climbed the rafters,
poured gallons of water
into each other's apartments
in a water fight that lasted
until our respective parents
returned from work and cut
our tails as the local parlance

referred to as an all-round beating
with anything to hand, a belt,
a little stick, an open hand.
We yelped and howled,
we were simply guarding
the house, next door started it
first and we had to finish it.
Mum stuffed old newspaper
in the cracks in the wall.

We moved after her
lover who drove a Pontiac
and weighed 350 pounds,
arrived one afternoon and
in front of everyone – every
tenement empty right then
to catch the late afternoon cool –
kicked an empty tin can,
his leg shot out from under
him like a revelation, a piston,
for a moment he became
a ballerina about to begin
a pirouette, a fine kick that sent
tin can clattering for yards,
but he dropped onto the concrete
and he rolled first to one side
then another to build up speed
and he swivelled onto one knee
and pushed off the ground
back onto his feet, but produced
such raucous and relentless
laughter in the tenement yard
for days and such shame
in us, that only a move could
quell, not fighting or any
kind of chant or spell.

Guyana Dreaming *Wilson Harris*

An explorer, he deposited me in his skull,
folded, tucked me away at the back part,
deep in a closet or bottom drawer in a chest
full of such drawers. I felt sure he buried me
just to forget me. Occasionally, light flicked
my way, or his mind's eye brushed past me.
Most times I lay surrounded by more
useful things or things he had more time for.

I almost gave up reasoning why I came up
short in his world, set aside for the time being
for the right time, but for now in my night time
waiting for the ripe time to make my entrance.
Something to do with his sense of himself
as casting shadows, instead of living under them,
made him remember me in his prison; or else
he dreamed me while he dozed in his lover.

Both suited me, twin reminders of him in two
minds about everything. He made me his ensign
when I preferred petals tightened into a bud.
Never mind. A dream cannot choose a dreamer.
A dream cannot even choose the occasion for
its making or when to make the occasion
chosen for its reality. The first thing I learned
in my state: patience. I watched, more listened.

I did not remind him of my presence. He knew.
That may be why he seemed worth the dream.
When he dreamed me he behaved as if ready
for what I promised. He merely provided room,
board for me at no cost to me and some worry
to his good self (the other being not so good).
I reminded him that I was the dream and he
The dreamer (or the other way round, or not).

Did he listen? Could I do more to win him over?
I knew my moment would come when he cast
his usual long shadow, walked with a bounce,
found himself in the open before either of us
could think. Chaos reigned. I behaved exactly
as a dream should. I sprang. Nightmares fled.
He dreamed me up and put me away then I made
my entrance; his exit; our contiguous worlds.

Local Colour

Dawn fills eyes and head and belly
A donkey in one field a tractor in another and a house in between
Flour sacks ripped open and sewn into dress and trousers
Pork barrels knocked to free the last morsel of pork lodged in them
Rain drops so large and individual they stone earth and us
A sun sticks at noon all day in a bleached sky
The log across a stream for a footbridge disguised as an alligator
The tsetse fly biplane and the helicopter seed
One loose paling on an otherwise perfect fence that everyone
                                                    ducks through
This man trapped under an overturned cart severs his leg to free
                                                    himself
That woman drops her child in a ricefield and picks up planting
                                                    where she left off
The grandmother takes the child and makes the woman taste the
                                                    afterbirth
How the child knows rice better than any schooled planter
The shell pond with coins in its eyes and a bed of precious stones
The fortuneteller who walks backwards and drinks methylated spirits
The ancient widow worms her way through keyholes to suck life
                                                    from babies
Fruits with a promise and a seed in the middle for chewing
A full moon draws near to listen to a child's whisper
Paddy bags stuffed with hay for a mattress shared on floorboards
One more bedtime story in a round of stories before insects fall quiet
A heart crawls in the body's crawlspace to take up residence in the
                                                    skull
The evicted contents of the skull settle in the empty chest

Succession

i.m. Lillian Dalton

I hand my life over to you
Embrace this gift for what it is
A raft of nights afloat in days

Elegies

Part One

1

I wake on Monday morning to my worst nightmare
Dirty blond sunshine making me squint on my drive
Home-to-the-office as I call my days spent there

Deleting email, returning calls and watching live
Feed of the latest from Iraq whose mounting dead –
Their drawn, bloodless faces and wide, watery eyes

Pleading to camera lens – fill my scabrous head.
I stare at Blacksburg's hills jutted against the sky
Drawing my office blinds and beat those hills

To the draw, their slouch matches my stance
Behind my desk, where I prepare to sit still,
Chained all day to tenure's incremental advance,

From the academic cradle to the academic grave,
I cut and paste coupons of my achievements and press Save.

2

Sudden sirens invade my office or what I hear as
Giant wasps in keeping with my primal fear: ambulance,
Fire, and police; I cannot think until they pass.

But they do not stop their panicky advance,
Drilling into my skull. I peel my lazy eyes off
My jittery computer screen to peer through

Slats in the blinds and I meet the passive/aggressive scoff
From studio backdrop hills and a brick wall of blue.
I ask a student, dressed in black from head to toe,

Liming in the corridor as she waits on a late professor,
What she knows about the sirens, since students know
Or always seem to be in the know like hip confessors

Of the urban apocalypse, for all my learning, all my hip,
Derives from the little bits I glean from reading their lips.

3

She wears silver on most of her ears, another rung
In her left nostril, and when she speaks, I count yet
Another ring, more like a stud, in the bed of her tongue.

She says there was a shooting at sunrise or sunset
(She could not be sure when) in one of the dorms.
I perk up, thank her and dash back to my laptop

Whose cursor, stuck where I left it, might be a hookworm
In a hurry or an index finger curled and uncurled or a Cyclops'
Eye winking some come-on, some endless invitation

For me to browse in its windows and not necessarily buy
Anything beyond the white sheet peregrinations
Of the LCD screen firing its blank airless sigh:

A cyber imperative that tells me I can be faceless too
Like everyone stuck to those screens by the same scentless glue.

4

Those sirens multiply. I wish more wax
Stuck in my ears, for once heard there's no unhearing
An emergency, no way to pretend; you can't relax

Any more, not with the nervous system rearing
Adrenalin, its chemical chime of anticipation,
Like the shook harness off that horse in Joyce's *Araby*.

I scour the headlines and find a message from
The campus police about two shot in their dormitory.
I Google the University for more than this polite notice,

While those sirens keep building a wedding cake of sound.
I know there is more. I slice open the door to my office
To find the decorated girl gone and no one else around.

I zoom back to the Web for any news of what's going on
In my immediate vicinity, since I cannot trust the song

And dance of my senses. Then I hear a loudspeaker
Asking everyone to remain indoors and stay away
From the windows and I know for sure it's a shooter;

Know that this would be no ordinary Monday.
I try the mobile but it's down, the company's motto
(I won't name them and provide free publicity) in TV ads

Is, *Can you hear me now?* And the answer's no.
I dash aside the mobile in disgust and grab
The landline to call home for news, but the wire

Connected to the handset is so tangled, like a snake
Curled up in a crazy knot, that the entire
Clumsy contraption falls like a stale pound cake,

Off my desk and chimes on the floor. I almost hurl
The phone but make the mouthpiece complete a Dervish whirl

6

Until the knots are exhausted, then I dial my house.
I ask, *Something's going on here, please tell me what?*
What I catch makes me swear like a Jamaican, *Blouse*

And skirts! I beg to hear it a second time so that
Repeated, the information might stick like a burr,
They say there are more than twenty fatalities

And it's the *fatalities* part that I never hear
Right, thinking it must be they mean to say injuries,
But no, I clock, fatalities, a third time, and just then

The laptop shows the same number and the corridors
Light up with staff, administrators, teachers and students
Looking at each other with that completely floored,

Open-mouthed, goldfish look, with eyes of a deer,
Locked on headlights, and a shortage of this thin air.

7

We duck into the open as instructed and head
Straight for parked cars; join long queues of vehicles
Peeling away from campus and very little said

Except for the murmur of idling traffic and bicycles
Eating up tarmac in that way students rough them up,
Throwing their weights around before their bodies head south.

No loud dance hall, no indy, no heavy metal, no rap,
None of the sounds the middle-aged complain about
Blaring from students whose purchasing powers

The music industry; only a silence whose fabric we
Scissor through with threaded tyres.
I collect the kids early from school and SUV

Home to even worse news coming from VT
I sit glued with the rest of the country to the TV.

8

Not twenty but thirty-two innocents killed, just think,
Thirty-two mown down in classrooms by weapons
You can buy legally before you can legally drink.

Flags at half-mast, funeral music on hit parade stations,
Everyone in black or Tech colours, ribbons on lampposts
In town, restaurant menus offer special condolences,

Students mill around, hug each other, some look lost,
Others search for the missing and ignore journalists' lenses
Thrust at them as the names of the dead begin

To trickle in, some learn about dead friends in Facebook
And MySpace and commemorate them by Instant Messaging:
Cyber prayers in virtual cathedrals by this most wired lot;

While the dead lie in mortuaries, their names and faces shine
Through optic fibres and satellite feeds for all time.

9

I meet one of my students face to face. Her red eyes, drained
Dry, make four with mine. She asks if I heard about Erin.
What about her? I know what she will say but before I complain,

No, more a moan than a protest, she says, Erin's gone, Sir.
I see her desk three desks back in that first row where she dived
For cover, like the rest of the class she always sat in one spot

Every time, so much so that I said one morning I'd arrive
Early and rearrange the desks and confuse them to bits.
What will we do come Tuesday when we meet as usual

But Erin's desk will be empty? I see her loping way
Of crossing a room. An athlete, she moves off the basketball
Court with so much economy for her strong body, as if space

In which she did not compete, hardly merited movement,
Like a coiled spring, off duty, or a loved government.

10

In our last exchange she took her friend's essay
And promised to deliver it. I said, Don't look at the grade,
Just in case it's better than the one I gave you. Without missing

A beat, she replied that whatever grade she made,
She intended to improve on it in the next assignment.
Erin, that would be the script written in the sky by a hand

More powerful than any pen I might wield over its firmament.
Erin, your grade would be 'A' for honour and over-standing.
There is no better grade than character and no bigger brass

Or wage to make than making a difference in this world.
Your name will last with all of us in that Caribbean class
For as long as we think and our tongues work.

Erin, queen of the court and brightest light in the room,
You are a bride now and death is your bridegroom.

11

That should be enough if this were a made up story but reality
Rivals any story ever told so much so we have to water
It down to make it fly with the reader and this is what really

Happens next. I find out the name of the shooter
And remember him from three meetings we had in my office
As part of a tutorial, after he was ejected from Poetry by the
                                                    professor

Who was right to throw him out. But he fell into my space
And will rent room in my head for the rest of my days. For
As long as I can think I will wonder if I could have seen

Something in him to ring an alarm and get him treated.
But I swear he showed nothing but extreme,
Stubborn, shy, idiosyncratic retreat.

He held his tongue as one holds onto a precious thing
So I could only guess his real thoughts from his writings.

12

I walk the Drillfield and see its many open wounds
Waiting for time to do its barely perceptible work,
Slow as the crawl of that sun across the blue sound,

That it paints and erases and paints once more,
Interrupted in its work by cloud and the canvas-
Slashing rain, but sure to be back after a storm

Where those thirty-two souls may be found in a vast
Sky shared by sun and rain and a double rainbow
With colours for each of the dead looped and unfolding,

From one end of the Roanoke Valley to another;
And for each life lost there's a fabled pot of gold
At the end of those rainbows; and for us left here

To witness that gift of rain and wealth of sun,
We know this week is not the end but new life begun.

Part Two

1

The sky curves a little closer, sun lights less
Harsh on our eyes, these mountains huddle
Around us, and trees bend with their shade.

Deer tiptoe in backyards, birds flick and dart
Without their usual squawks, only the breeze
Whispers about those missing in its fingertip talk.

This town of our new and mass dead
Plucked from our lives by a blind pair of hands,
Hums with the traffic of lost souls,

Twists to the tune of our macular grief,
Sleeps little and light with one eye open,
Picks at food like a frightened canary.

This is Blacksburg back on its feet,
Back in the groove, Blacksburg undefeated.

2

More than my cup, in your hand, raised
To your lips, for a sip of the Caribbean,
Is the single rose cut for your grave.

More even than words from minds
Held under lamps kept burning round
The clock is the sting in my eyes that blinds.

Less of you in my head with each day,
Not the lessening of desire but hope
Lost, not the growth of amnesia but prayer,

And not to a god in the sky or inside
But some thing whose rays emanate from
What is left of you in what I keep with pride:

Keep and do not crush in a hardback book;
Cherish but not smother with too hard a look.

3

I sleep on a mattress stuffed with bones,
Human bones;
My head on a pillow filled with hair,
Human hair;
A bed made with black and white sheets of skin,
Human skin;
Floats down a river of soup-like blood,
Human blood;
Flows into a sea of dead flesh,
Human flesh;
Sinks to the bottom of that soundless sea,
Human sound.
Settles there with me grafted to it,
Human dark.

4

My skull carries all the dreams of all those bones.

The country I'm in is the country of their birth.

Its hills roll like they rolled their shoulders.

Its valley can be traced down any one of their backs.

I count the bones of thirty-two lost souls, no, thirty-three,

And wear their hair on my head and on my back.

The four seasons of this land roll into one season

Of no sun and no moon to speak of.

Only what light wakes before my eyes slingshot open

Light that looks the same with my eyes closed.

Only a dream of snow I made into snow angels,

And leaves I buried myself in, and summers

When I was lazy as pollen,

When a day slept after lunch for the rest of the afternoon.

5

All the nerves in my body pulled from me
And wrung into a tight plait so all the blood falls from them.

All those nerves hung on a line in a brash sun
Until they wither into strings.

All those strings as delicate as a web,
So delicate that they crumble

In a child's careless fingers.
All that wringing as if on a rack

And that drying in a direct flame.
None of it

Conveys how numb
How like a shocked thing,

How stunned April 16th left me
So that now is exactly like then till kingdom come.

6

Till kingdom come or another Beelzebub with more
Ambition and a new pointless record of dead.

Madman more like. Manmade as much
As anything. I forgive you

Though I cannot forget what you have done.
I have no time for you, not until

Memory and imagination serve
Your victims – what they did and what

They planned to do, and what I imagined
Them doing with their families and friends.

Then perhaps, someday, sometime, you and
Your bloodline will take up room in my mind.

Until then get to the back of the line,
And bide your self-extinguished time.

Part Three

1

Police speckle campus lawns, their cars parked
Ostentatiously, illegally, public exhibits
In an open-air museum of broken hearts.

Their gun-metal charm sets me on edge.
The ones in plain clothes stand out even more,
Their inconspicuous intent is itself conspicuous.

Bless them for their crude cover of us in our raw state.
We believe in nothing but slowness when in the open,
For the sun as it slips cloud cover, startles with its glare.

And no man, woman or child looks quite so lost,
As when left to idle before an impromptu memorial,
By an impulse that stays one step ahead of thinking.

What am I thinking when I catch my self in its stasis?
That love's cloak keeps us warm in a crisis.

2

That the sun had no malicious intent until now,
As we move in our skin-scrubbed-raw condition,
Our eyelids peeled back to show too much white,

Our feet sore from walking on shingle
That fell like rain all over town while some
Army sneaked in and took away our shoes.

Some of us walk on our hands for comfort
Others tiptoe and the people in pairs give
Each other piggybacks – better one pair of feet

Than two, better still if this sun can be turned
Back to a time when the half moons of fingernails
Kept us busy, and the big picture was a CNN catastrophe:

A man going over Niagara Falls in a barrel;
A medical team undoing the reef knot of conjoined twins.

3

I avoid the news in all its formats and stick
With friendly testimony, tongues grow
Wild as vines watered by rumour run wild.

Truth is mugged, hardly a mugging, a baby
Whose only true possession, innocence,
Cannot be taken away, though something's lost:

An image of a youngster at the start of a road
That twists out of sight, and all those springy
Legs need do is embark on this life journey.

That's gone, for an image of a road with chasms
So deep that long lines of youth surge down
Unawares, and their parents look on helplessly.

We count the cost afterwards, astonished at the toll;
The roads that lead, not to long lives, but early burials.

4

There was a joke about the shooter students
Loved to tell, before it blew up in their faces:
Did you hear the one about... that I can't repeat

Here and desecrate the names of the fallen.
Humour sits next to prediction, the two occupy
Sides of a coin thrown into the middle of lives

Without knowing which lands face up, and us
Face the consequence, in this case a lone man
In a VT hat and reflective shades plotting

His glory at a price many among us pay
For with our lives, and the rest of us left
With a gamble, ask, what are the chances

That this would happen here and now,
In a county where people barely outnumber cows?

5

The last time I laugh without checking my
Laughter at the door of abandonment, laugh
Unbridled, is the morning of the sixteenth

Before I catch up with the news and get
Caught up in it. I tell a colleague the story
From my secondary school days of a friend

Who pulls up his fly zip with automatic zeal
And catches a piece of himself in the zip
And none of us, in stitches, helps him

With it and he ends up going to the emergency,
Where a nurse he fancies, manhandles him,
And frees him from his misery and he boasts

That he stirs with lust for her as she touches him
Instead of the boy we leave with her that's screaming.

6

I tell this now to show the light years of events
Before and after that date and how when I laugh
At anything there's a sour taste left in my mouth,

Whose corners, turned up for laughter, could just
As easily flip into the mask I wear just beneath
Every expression; that tinges everything I do,

From picking up my child to when my partner
Takes the bulk of me in her hand and loads me
Into her, when all the children sleep,

When the whole house settles into its foundation,
On a hill settled, in turn, in its mineral bed; we rock
Each other to a crescendo we keep muted,

Not to wake the house, not to stir the dead,
Who line up in neat rows in my shaved head.

How can I feel this itch, now, and, actually,
Scratch it, rather than keep such urges
Under raps? I recoil from that someone in me

Who looks like me in a hardhat armed with
Pen and paper, looking on at my life,
Calling what he does art, while seemingly

Lacking a heart. Who holds his child's soft
Head in his palms and thinks of a fruit
Dashed against concrete, in a banana republic,

Or housing project, or behind the dark windows
Of the house next door. Or any place where
Flesh loses its value, so that when held,

He feels nothing but a burden, or bundle
On his back or chained to his best ankle.

Memory works that way too, and ambition.
At this moment I am all memory, freighted by
Names and faces picked out from a crowd

Randomly. They were transported here
At fridge temperature and released in the open:
Brush-tailed butterflies dropped on campus

For safe keeping, so delicate that powder
Shed when you brushed against their separates
Worn lightly in classrooms. That's how the young

Seem to me, from my middle-aged bunker:
Delicate as butterflies, with a butterfly's agility;
Ready to alight on any surface that holds promise.

All their camouflage colours could not save them,
Nor my wish to shield them from the gun's flame.

9

This morning lifts in the valley, or descends,
If light fruits on trees, or falls as light rain;
Heaves lead weights off my shoulders, or at least

Falls in step with my step, and shares the burden,
Planted there since the sixteenth, that blossomed,
So that relief resembles excavation,

When what I wanted, ideally, looked more like
How the day begins, without trace, and takes
Root in my gaze and supplants darkness,

Leaving me unburdened, enlightened,
Grateful for my calendar's relentless
March from one end of my study to another:

Shadows crossing the floor, beams afloat
In dust, and my student's face in those floats.

10

I found a four-leaf clover, for the first time
In twenty years of pottering around gardens,
On three continents, in a bed of thyme,

I doubled over to pick a sprig for my spaghetti
Sauce recipe that's a family secret, kept by the tines
Of forks, and passed from hand to mouth.

I meant to press it right away in a tome,
Kept by my bed, but I answered the phone
And forgot about the clover and it shrivelled,

Doubled over, and looked unlike anything
Seen in a garden. I should follow my mind.
I wanted to ignore the ringing but did not.

I got a telemarketer who wanted to sell me life
Insurance. I need a policy for death. I hung up.

11

Not the mint planted on the slant lawn
For a whiff of Mahaicony when I cut June grass,
But the blade of the mower that mulches

Greenery, butterflies, ants, wasps and mint.
Not my child lowered on grass for the first time
To sit and stare and pull at each curved blade,

But the measure of that child under that ground.

Stop at that precipice or lose your mind.

Some things if imagined too long come
About, brought into being by the seed of thought,
As if finding a portal into life provided

By that thought process, therefore I banish
All impulse and imagery of my child
As anything but an adult and me in my dotage.

Part Four

1

The film rights for this event feel wrong,
For now, the idea sounds vulgar like a bar joke
Told in the catacombs. Hollywood turns on

Automatic transmission, free of restraint,
Guided by satellite and cable, rather than sin,
Or bad taste, so assume the race started

For a script on the seventeenth, over lunch,
Pitched by a writer to a cadre of producers,
With a menu said to serve the victims.

But only those around the table eat till full.
They leave flushed with the wine of possibility,
Not since Titanic; the Hindenburg...

Use my skin for papyrus, for a lampshade,
Dip my hollowed bone in my blood for ink.

2

For the war effort the government requisitions
All metals in all households, principally guns,
And the casings of ammunition, all types

Of guns, so that the entire state and union
Is denuded of private arms and its citizenry
Walk about empty-handed and misaligned for not

Bearing the posture-held gait of someone
Packing a ballistic punch. I dream on behalf
Of the dead yesterday, today and tomorrow.

We export death better than we manage it
On the domestic market. A massacre on campus
Stuns us the way a suicide bomber in Baghdad

Can never do, beyond our quest to maintain
Our rising dead, added to a range of mountains.

3

After J.B.

Tap drum, slap its body; beat out drum blood melody:
Tum-tum ba-dam, tum-tum ba-dam, biddy-bip
Biddy-bip, tum-tum-ba-dam.

Wake drum, make drum talk and laugh like you happy:
Tum-tum ba-dam, tum-tum ba-dam, biddy-bip
Biddy-bip, tum-tum-ba-dam.

Goat-skin drum, sheep-skin drum, cow-skin drum,
Obeah man drum, medicine woman drum,
African, Irish, Indian and Asian drum.

Soul, funk, rock, rap, pop and punk drum,
Tum-tum ba-dam, tum-tum ba-dam, biddy-bip
Biddy-bip, tum-tum-ba-dam.

Tum-tum ba-dam, tum-tum ba-dam, biddy-bip
Biddy-bip, tum-tum-ba-dam.

4

After Lord Kitchener

Blacksburg is the town for me,
Boo-do-do-do, boo-do, pa-pom, pa-pom;
Blacksburg, small town in big country.

If you go to Hong Kong, or Cuba,
Iraq, Afghanistan or Grenada,
You must come back to Blacksburg and VT.

Don't believe me come for yourself and see,
Is not my April 16th grief turned love joy talking,
I taught at Bates, Amherst, the University of Miami,

Newcastle, Durham and Cambridge;
None offered this mountain and village combo;
So I'm happy in Blacksburg at VT.

Boo-do-do-do, boo-do, pa-pom, pa-pom
Boo-do-do-do, boo-do, pa-pom, pa-pom.

Part Five

1

Young bodies sport dictionaries,
But none transcribe to their tongues,
None lend print to fingers licked

Before pages stick, crackle and turn
Over for minds that plunder them for what
Light these etymologies shed and peel

Back to reveal, back to a time before
Print, before tongues fell flat in mouths
As eyes took root in minds, and minds

Grew eyes and tongues lost their forks
And fell flat on their faces and acted
Blind to pages that made tongues thick:

Drowned books in a shipwreck of spines,
Hulls made of ribs, decks covered with skins.

2

I stared at my students through Plexiglas
Thick as a vault door and they stared back,
Foreheads grazing the apparent wall of sea.

I pressed my hands to clear plastic to show
Empty hands, no weaponry: how
They studied my palms; they seemed

To read them, and find out something
About me best left unsaid, sight unseen.
They drifted away from me, just as

Cows graze a pasture without a map.
But in this aquarium of my dream,
Need refuses to enter the lexicon:

All eyes absorb flashbulbs, mouths
Speak in perfect, thought-bubble O's.

3

Today campus life revolves around
Ceremonies for those about to leave us,
And some who left before their time.

Our shadows belong to the missing,
Sundials that circle our feet, as we traverse
The Drillfield's hub and the spokes

Of pavement, where notice boards
Tell us what to think about our loss.
Silence and nothingness disappear

Just when you need them, leaving us
Burdened with throwaway greet-
ings, and maybe a chance-hug, or glance,

From someone who understands
Why our shadows labour under our feet.

4

I borrowed her pen to write a code
Dictated to me over the campus phone.
The four digits unlocked a cabinet

Full of audio-visual goodies. I showed
Sugar Cane Alley and we discussed
How memory and history work in the film.

Out of the blue, I was back in that classroom
With a memory of her thick among us, and no way
To tie our history with any project other than life,

And no means of redress, for she was gone,
Leaving a number with a ring to it when
I think how I asked her for that pen,

And how she handed it over without
Touching me and not a word from her mouth.

5

My mum cooked soul food for my final class:
Fried plantains, cow-tail in a stew of casareep,
Boiled dumplings, sliced pineapple and mango

Juice, for our first meeting after the cancelled week.
One student arrived with a bouquet for my mother.
Everyone heaped *Pirates of the Caribbean* paper plates

For this breakfast, minus one of our number, gone
For good. We ate as if on the heels of a Ramadan
Squeezed into a week of nil by mouth, ears and eyes.

My mum flew into Blacksburg for our joint offer.
She rose before the birds and I helped to skin
Exotica and washed up to keep the kitchen clean.

At 9am we breezed into my Caribbean class
And served up honeydew with plates of paradise.

6

There is no wrong she can do from this day on.
All my gripes with her nursed over decades
Withered away with this one visit and single act.

Mother, who multiplied loaves and fish, turned
Waters of distress into wines of contentment,
Mother, who parted the sea of despair for dry land.

(I should stop but I can't, won't, not now)
Mother who picked a flower in the West Indies
And planted it again in the Hebrides

Where the flower grew thorns around it
So that it would be hard to move again.
But Mother also grew a glove around her skin

And she picked that flower and moved it
To the United States and sunk its roots in coral.

Part Six

1

Remember a time in your life when
A rose was a rose in anything but name.
Remember that redness in sunlight,

That perfume that filled the wide open
Museum of your days and nights.
How you thought it would never end.

Well, my quarrels seemed that way
Up until then, carefully brought to boil,
Then turned down to simmer on a low

Flame of just retribution. Until that time,
When all else shrunk to a pinpoint
And the rose was ground to floating dust,

And only the raw blood of the dead in the air
And only their cell phones for bees around flowers.

2

Now I walk gingerly with slivers in both
Heels, the balls of my feet, and in each
Big toe. I no longer watch where I place

My foot, so much as place each foot with
A minimum of my weight on that leg,
Perfecting the art of distributing my weight

Between my steps and in air not breathed
On this temporal earth, so that I weigh less
Than my body and defy the very gravity

I swear my name by, to cuddle its magnetism,
As one would a wasp hoping it won't sting,
Just because it's shut in by walls of juicy flesh:

And so I step one foot placed before the next
And go from class to office in a murdered context.

3

I met a man dressed in black from head to toe.
His forehead sported a cap, pulled so low
His eyes could have been open, shuttered

Behind reflective shades. He said little, lingered
A lot, wanting something or not much.
He did not stand out in a crowd, unless you

Thought a man dressed like that, who hovered,
Merited attention. He did not. Students
Find limitless ways to catch a teacher's eye.

Take the drama major who wore different
Coloured socks and sneakers every time
I saw him, and who must have paired his socks

And shoes deliberately wrongly to create an effect
Of a dorm shared by two people each with one leg.

4

Or one man with two heads, splitting one body.
A man in two minds about himself, or with many
Selves to account for one body and several

Shades of mind. A man who can only guess,
Who cannot begin to know what he may
Be today until he squares off with a mirror

Beckoning him into its silvered surface that acts
As a door into one of those persons bubbling
Inside and dying to get out and leave his mark

On a world that barely recognises one self,
Never mind two or more. That man plucks
Out his eyes and wears a blindfold for effect.

He feels his way to class, to a full room
Splintered from his body pulling him to his doom.

5

If he kills one or all he restores whoever looks
Out from behind those shades. If he stops
The proliferation of himself spreading out of his

Sight and mind he stops his own dissipation.
He would erase his own shadow to begin with.
Then turn to involuntary twitches and shudders,

For they denote lack of self control and then
Graduate to attack the flesh of others who
Resided once in his head and now walk away

From him as if he was not worth a second
Look and therefore in need of one final act
To grab attention even if that means an end

To the self that thinks for the man in black,
Hat low in his eyes and shades for a blind.

6

I promised I would not spend any time
On the probable inner workings of the mind
Of a man who butchered so many people.

I wanted all my energy to devote itself
To honouring the names and memories
Cut down in their prime for nothing.

I began and found I could not separate
Him from them because he too was in
His prime, and though his hand made

The cuts, he was among the slaughtered.
Thus I find myself thinking about his loss
And theirs as multiple sides of a prism:

Whatever light shines in comes out unequal.
Whatever light comes out, forms an equation.

7

Analogies rarely work in poetry but here's one:
Parents each take an arm of their lovechild,
Sandwiching her, and walk her in an effort

To teach her how to walk since she wants to
Walk before her time, and in this act of mimicry
They hope to draw the real thing from her.

Question: Are they wrong to instil such ambition
In one so young? The question never occurred
To them. They walked their baby who showed

Interest in perambulation, not as a crawl-before
You-walk progression, but as missing one stage
For the final desired end. Call it what you want,

Nothing alters the image of those two with the little
Person of their pooled genes ensconced in the middle.

8

Parents who bury a child keep something
Resembling that image inside, but never dream
They'd retrieve it so soon for their lost offspring.

They miss pictures of grandchildren to go with
This earliest memory, at a table laden with three
Courses, around which this very story is told;

And perhaps a toast to chase that story down
Into flesh of the teller's flesh and so on.
But not this abrupt end and the last thing

Is among the first things, in an end to accumulating
Precious bits and pieces that add up to the puzzle
Of a life lived, the best way we know how,

In a time we cannot control, whose tests
Surprise us, like a coffin with our future laid to rest.

Part Seven

1

When I first drove through Downtown,
Blaring 'Brown-Eyed Girl' by Morrison
In that hired U-haul packed with tropical

Plants from seven years in Miami's oven,
Flora destined to perish that first winter,
I thought Blacksburg, curled up between hills,

Resembled a kitten snuggled into a large sofa.
I heard the purrs of contentment in 5 o'clock
Traffic forming a neat line at one traffic light

Gracing High Street and saw the town
As that kitten curling around a lamp-post
At the feet of pedestrians who outnumber cars.

My allergy to felines evaporated. I stopped, killed
The stereo, and petted that cat from whisker to tail.

2

In early '80s London my then girlfriend
Never passed a cat in any street without a long
Hello and strokes that turned the feistiest

Felines into burbling fur balls – her habit drove
Me crazy with a mix of impatience and jealousy.
I wanted to be all those cats, rolled into one,

Earning her abandoned affection that defied
Time and space and discretion. I think of that
Now I am close to living with a cat

To please my children. I figure domestic
Cats as emblems of civilisation, just as this town,
Before that date, was one thing, and now,

It's another, wounded, but no less precious thing,
Able to wail, wallow, and someday sing.

3

Fishing at Pandapas Pond on a sunny Saturday
Morning with my children and new rods and bait
Dug from the garden that very morning,

Proved more taxing than two hours of sirens
Heard in a news blackout while trapped in my office.
I had to avoid flying hooks and steady wriggling

Worms onto their needle-sharp tips and wait
While the boys complained that nothing was happening
As nothing much happened to the float, except

An unsolicited image of a boy like them in Guyana
Holding a makeshift rod with twine kept afloat
By bottle cork, studying the end of that line

So hard that string above the water and below
Switched to two fishers, one out and one in The Know,

4

Unsure whether I was in or out of the drink
(Out suited me because the underwater version
Faced upwards with the pond's glass surface

Acting like a ceiling). The point at which perspective
Bifurcated, on the skin of the water, that entry point,
Separated the line into two distinct pieces.

The line in the water floated a little to the left
Of the line out of the water and the submerged
Line wavered like a water snake, whereas the line

From the rod formed a perpendicular angle of solid
Steadiness, and it was there that my eyes revolved
In my head to make me switch places with the fisher

In the water, who fished for men as the men chased
Fish, but who seemed to settle for my boy's face.

5

My gaze is certainly downward of late.
I keep seeing a trench packed with prostrates
As I called the dead in jest once and once only

Before I ever knew death would visit me
Willy-nilly with a laying-on of hands on my cranium,
Or a tap on my shoulder from a hand I never swivel

My head around fast enough to see, no matter
How quickly I move. Or an involuntary shudder
At the height of summer. Or a mass of deaths

In one act all around me, as if I were in a lottery,
A wheel spun or dice rolled, and each of us
That morning wore a number on those dice,

Or engraved on that wheel, that faced up
When the wheel stood still or the roll stopped.

6

Did a black cat cross my path as I drove to work
Monday, April 16th? Did a crow lap my house
Repeatedly on one wing beat? Did two bad events

Precede this third calamity, since sorrow comes
In threes? Did I commit some terrible act
In a past life that now sought recompense?

Did I kill too many living creatures as I ate,
Fished, mowed the lawn, stepped blindly
Through life? Did I dream of this when I woke

Shouting blue murder and could not recall
What made me thrash about in my sleep?
Did our brief contact add a hump to the killer's back?

I think these things without thinking, without deeds
They come unbidden into my wake and sleep.

Part Eight

1

My body in reverse motors food up
From the celery pit of my stomach
(Or should that be salary) since I

Serve a broker whose ledger balances
Goggle-eyed zeros and crosses,
(Or should that be google) numbers

For birth, crucifixes for graves, in fields
Devoid of dreams, guarding untimely
Dead (that should be dreams deferred) who

Inspire a surfeit of platitudes, and just for
Saying that, a scalpel cuts inside my head,
One slash for each dead, a wound

Behind my eyes, as deep as those dead,
Not easily drained or dredged.

2

S-Joe marched up and down Lamaha Street daily
Backwards; Sabbatic drank methylated spirits until
She spontaneously combusted; Walker the Nigger

When called by that name replied British you fool;
Bolo could not keep a stitch on his body in public;
Star Boy wet his khaki trousers and stank to high heaven.

These mud head people from my past in Guyana
Come back to me when I wonder how they might be
If dead in that capital bundled on the edge of a continent

Below sea level with a crumbling seawall.
None of those characters prepared me for this
Not one of them could do a thing like this

In posited moments of clarity each offers
Praise to the dead, commiserations to survivors.

3

How will they distill in my mind?
Will they zoom at me in a zigzag, spiral,
Curve or loop-the-loop recollection?

What if they never change their funeral
Apparel for campus gear in my inspections?
When will I remember them? At what time

Day or night? Why can't I pick
The hour and place as one would a fight
Or love session? Where do I stick

Them? In my head or heart, and, if
Both, then how to decide the split?
I balk at an image of someone like me

Stuck in the cereal aisle, like a brick,
Wet-faced, unable to retrieve the word for tea.

4

Which brings to mind Polish Piotr's dilemma.
Brought to America before the wall collapsed
We cut him loose among 57 varieties of cereals,

He returned from the megastore, empty-handed,
Shaking his head at the glut of choice, and unable,
Therefore, to buy any food except unfiltered cigarettes.

Let me think of the dead when I am with friends
Who shared the heavy parcel of that Monday,
And will carry it, gift-wrapped, to our various ends.

The press packed up long ago and moved on
To another disaster. The police scaled down
Patrols and the public deluge is now a trickle,

Us left hands full and lost in this fleeced landscape
Of proliferating memorials and yellow police tape.

5

Legal counsel for those left on the perimeter of grief
Involves retained Rottweilers that patrol our property.
We throw them our rights; they guard against litigious thieves.

We sleep sound and dream of the dock and a jury
Loaded against us like the good old, bad old days of the South.
No warm beakers there. No white sands issuing its tide

Of invitation to our winter bodies. Only the ulcerated
Tongue wagging in a mouth which talks out of the side
Of a two-faced man in a crest on the bench ready

With his gavel to come down hard on the side of power.
Oh polemic, chewing away at my art, and holding your
Breath until I take notice, please let me be for one stanza,

Pure as the reign of peace on a Tibetan mountain,
Easy as cottage smoke, true as light from a stained

6

Moon leaning in a bedroom window to form
Lake Placid on that Scotchguard carpeted floor.
I ask, hat in hand, head bowed, knee ready to genuflect.

Don't ask me to kiss your feet as I would Guyana's
Soiled ground were I to fly back there heralded
For art for art's sake and no other politic reason.

I ask as a man with only one trick to his name:
An art with no rulebook to speak of, and no government
But the tongue and its twist of lemon and lime

As a way in this stellar world. I ask, finally,
As a father who wishes his children safe passage
In a voyage where I am left standing on the jetty

Waving at a pinpoint, on the horizon, coloured whisky,
Until there is no point where a flat-lined sea meets sky.

Part Nine

1

We consecrate them to ground
Turned over for a yield we wait
In line to join. Our prayers sound

Automatic issued at heaven's gate,
Built by hands that steer our heads
Away from seeing that dig as more

Like something with us planted, seeds
Ended there for a start we can't know
Anything about in our altered state,

Breathing our last before a witness
Who loves us rather than hates
Flesh for no reason he can express:

This after hearing his garbled message
Aired before we buried those he wasted.

2

No man up above to invest in,
No smart force in this universe
To leave acts I cannot explain.

No place to go after I perish
But the grave or my ashes sown
Over the Demerara which catapults

Into the Atlantic which flows
Back, back, back, to Africa
Where ancestors walked head-in-air,

But earlier they dragged knuckles
There, and were captured there,
And packed in ships in shackles:

An old story without a loving God
A bone I throw to polemic, my dog.

Who must be fed no matter what
I say, or how I say it, or why.
Polemic, whose bite is its bark;

One hoarse and bloodcurdling cry;
Whose habits run riot in my veins,
Like now, as blood from so many

Good people around me stains
Floors and walls, as we keep company
With grief, and follow its hearse.

That could be why when the impulse
Kept on a leash and quelled, bursts
From me I let it run its wily course:

Too many dead in one small place,
To lower my head or cover my face.

4

Too many fallen, too close to breathe,
Without smelling my own mortality,
In every chance encounter, beneath

Every smile I meet menace daily,
Plastered on faces worn like masks,
Stitched to heads torn between

Wake and sleep: awake in a nightmare,
Adrift the big sleep, painted damask,
Left to cake into a shrill sheen,

A see-through smile, a bony stare,
Trigger-finger against my temple
In mock slaughter in cold blood:

So like PS3 that obliterates sample
Peoples, demolishes neighbourhoods.

5

That finger was never the real thing,
No comparison, but it left an imprint
Whose burn is ancestral, whose sting

Replays and never stops collecting rent
From my kind, when that fingerprint
Is white and the marked skin is black.

I wish I were making this up,
But this is history and fact,
Intermingled, that says *don't fuck*

With us unless you have thick skin
And broad shoulders, we flick a whip
Measuring time in waves and particles.

We keep prisoners for life in cells
Of their own making and we celebrate.

6

They dance on our graves, they traipse
Roads of our bones, they pluck hearts,
Beating, from children, as one picks grapes.

This much sought after delicacy starts
Their menu, that ends with harvested souls,
Chased down with cauldrons of blood.

I dreamed this gothic unedited whole-
Sale that stuck to my eyes like crud
I could not wash off with any element

On the periodic table, the kind that grows
On you so when you glance at the firmament
You see your face in a blizzard of stars.

Your face multiplied to the nth degree;
You, the killer and those killed make three.

Part Ten

1

America wakes up with a headache
Since America feels tired from thinking
How mineral and mental tectonic plates

Shift against American global rule
When a soldier from the Midwest
Falls to friendly fire and the cover up

Comes natural to those who would
Show the Iraq war as nothing less
Than necessary, nothing more than

Godly predestination. That's how
Bugles call by his grave for more young
To step forward and save the nation

On foreign soil before the fight
Comes to us, we take it to them, right?

2

Say it unadorned. An oil magnate
Spellbinds developed nations; oil separates
From water and oil splits peoples; the two

Won't mix or if they do heads roll
From the vestments worn by suicide
Bombers caught in that cocktail.

Save us all from ideas about nation
States; save us from arguments
Built on land surrounded by fences.

We came into this life defenceless
And will go out doors on gurneys
Whether we own dollars or cents.

Tell the circling hawk that garden mole
Limbo dances with grass on foreign soil.

3

Tell a parent to let go of their child
When that child should have borne them
Grandchildren and seen them (not they see

Her) out of this world. Such order defies
Chance, defies life's curveballs thrown
By hands that pitch at no one and everyone,

Regardless of stature, colour, piety.
This makes life a lottery and ambition
A knave as Shakespeare would put it.

But to wake without ambition would be
To surrender in this waking world to
The big sleep that rounds our little life.

That is how I see the many campus dead;
Circling unremittingly in my tenured head.

Then I see it differently as a new day
Affords a changed perspective on things.
Thanks to the long march of time,

I forget what I leave far behind.
I change my mind or hold both
Conditions to be true and cannot pick

One or other. Thanks to the firefly
Whose flight path, though lit,
Charts a zigzag path and no straight

Staying the course. I caught one once.
I closed my eyes and shut my left hand
In front of me and there it was,

Glowing in the prison of my palm,
X-raying my veins, showing my dead hand.

5

I uncurl my fingers in the night air,
The next thing I see is a thousand
Lights from as many fireflies as pinholes

In the pincushion black. I run back
Home with the children I share bedding
With on the floor when I hear my name

Shouted from a top floor window.
The last one home shuts the bottom
Half-door, the first one in wins

The biggest slice of baked bread
Ready for butter to skid off it,
Hardly chewed, and washed down

With a tin cup of tea and two sugars,
Tea cooled by separating two tin cups.

6

One dead student walked in my shoes,
I continue in thought where
Her death left off that April morning.

There is no better work in life than
Taking up the slack of someone
Whose grip was forced to slip and slide.

The work, just as hard, feels twice
As sweet as any job foisted on me.
And that's what I tell myself every

Morning as I approach my desk
And face its reproach that I dare
To advance on anything but my belly:

Prostrate before a being who with one
Look turns living things to cold stone.

7

Not one with snakes for dreadlocks,
That's too easy, but a woman who
Turns heads in a mall just by how

She puts one foot directly in front
Of the next and creates a pendulum
Swing of hips and balances an invisible

Fruit basket on her head, her long neck
Like a vase made by a Grecian with an
Eye on an ode to his work and posterity.

She comes towards me and I should
Keep my blindfold on as instructed,
But I feel her near and rip it off my eyes:

The rest you know, how she turns a population
Down, like a chambermaid, a bed, at the Hilton.

8

That media profile needs one enhancement:
The mall was closed to the public.
A café failed to lock its mall entrance

So we exited into a graveyard of shop
Windows and met a security guard
Who reached for his holster when he

Bumped into us on his ghostly rounds.
The end could have been bloody
If that guard had an eye on his fifteen

Minutes in the limelight, no matter
What colour the lens or how bright
The studios, instead he beckoned us

To the iron grid, lifted it for us to duck
Into streetlight and wished us good luck.

Part Eleven

1

For my usual early run in Jefferson
Forest, even outside hunting season,
I wear colours that proclaim, I am not

Deer or turkey or whatever else
The men in caps and fatigues chase,
More lie in wait for. I pass a sign

Whose prohibition acts like an open
Invitation: FINE FOR FISHING.
Hunters take it as a signal of fruitful

Endeavour and even plant a few rounds
Like kind breeze-cuts through the letters.
My orange gear looks nothing like deer

So I hope as I run a snaking track
Enveloped by a green tent with gashes

2

Cut with a scythe swung by a painter
Whose palette mixes green with blue.
Not so, says the burn in my lungs and legs

As I toil uphill for the wages of health
And unwind deeper into the woods
Past deer or squirrels rushing over fall's

Dry cellophane with a scrunch and tell-
Tale flash of white, until I come to my
Turning point, three miles from home, over

Looking Blacksburg, at the cell phone
Tower, newly planted among cleared trees.
And there I spot something that makes

My already rapid pulse sky
Rocket and my shallow breathing

3

Trip over itself for more bitter air:
Two men in pickups, in confabulation,
Who hardly seem to notice me

When I say morning and wave,
The one in a Panthers cap touches
His hat-rim as if adjusting it; the other

Makes a barely perceptible nod and I
Turn and run faster and harder to put
As much ground between them and me

As I can. I think if I hear an engine
I'll dive off the beaten track and head
For the nearest house or simply hide

In underbrush, and I plough on
Breathing loudly and grimacing.

4

Both of which I never do on these
Mornings when I affirm flesh will not
Fall foul of time, and early, dew-laced air

Constitutes the first meal of the day.
I try to listen above the scramble of pebble
Under my hasty steps, I even look back

That no one creeps up on me. Then I hear
The motor far off at first, then clamouring,
And I glance behind and see the dirt cloud

From too much speed on dry mud, and I
Peer into the trees and fight an impulse
To simply dive in among the thorns and

Crouch out of sight until they pass.
But I opt to stick to the trail and face them.

5

There's so much history between us.
I carry ammunition from a past
I do not own, but lay claim to.

Past names and dates and brutal acts
Left to fester in me, so when I meet
History, my eyelids peel back in shock.

History owns me, but owes me nothing.
History passes me in cities like a stranger.
When I hail History by name, I get no

Response, not even a distant look.
I try to catch up against the flow of foot
Traffic and bump shoulders and lose History,

As if History were deaf to my entreaty,
And therefore mute when it comes to me.

6

I stop and stand with arms akimbo,
As they pull alongside me I wave,
They nod as before and dash off a mock

Salute and pass me raising more dust
Than the hell I expected, that one or both
Would load a rifle to his shoulder and

Unleash some of what the history between
Our races liberally bequeathed us,
With me on the wrong end of the exchange.

This is April 16th speaking, when nothing
Normal can ever happen again without
A tinge of murderous intent lacing it.

For a man with guns could only be read
As one false move and you're dead.

Part Twelve

1

In my dream I see a man who hands
Out flowers to everyone he meets.
People accept his roses when they catch

His eyes and broad smile and before
They bow, bless, hail or enquire, what for,
He rushes to another surprised taker,

Until he runs out and skips back,
With the same smile on his face,
To his dorm, to load up with more.

So it goes until I wake with his
Same pleased look on him changed
By me for today when all the talk's about

How a man thrust flowers at everyone,
And before they thanked him he moved on.

2

Here comes a bouquet in the form of a man,
All that pollen makes him a magnet for bees,
They trail this ambulant garden campus

Wide as its stocks deplete and spreads
Joy for free, if someone says no to a flower
It's because this simply too kind act

Must come with a price tag, just as a bee
Swings with a sting in its tail, so a rose
Recalls a funeral parlour papered with petals

And music with the quiet persistence
Of a swarm in search of a home,
Emanating from its petalled walls.

That's how long I hold onto this image,
Before it wilts for his gun-toting visage.

3

Before the stems of roses switch to gun barrels
Aimed at everyone in sight and blossoms red
When grounded in flesh, before police tape

Fences lots he devastated, let me keep
Hold of my student late with her
Assignment, slouched in a swivel seat across

From me behind my desk as we examine her
Handiwork after an exchange of pleasantries
About the semester drawing to a close,

Let me keep her in my office past the sixteenth
Holed up in there in a marathon conversation
Neither of us ends for no reason we can name,

Other than the fact that outside a man wishes
To take her life that she's not ready to relinquish.

4

The same reality unfolds in thirty-two
Offices including one where the shooter
Forgets to walk out as he tosses around

A notion that the hills around campus
Remain romantic emblems any Wordsworth
Coleridge or Shelley would gawk at

Except bulldozers remove their tops
For what's inside and leave dirty piles
Where a forest once dressed a hill,

And for this the talk tries to reconcile
How to keep the hills and the machines
In the same poem without losing the feel

For nature as a force even when faced
With explosives and gutted by diggers.

5

He writes his way to extinction.
He puts down his gun and takes up a pen.
Laptop instead of notebook, files not pages.

He makes it to graduation with no idea
What to do next with his American life.
That was never a part of the dream,

But I think it on behalf of him as I do
For all the dead who left off thinking.
They queue in my head for a turn

At the wheel, the wheel's spin, their
Place on it as something more than
News items and them not there.

I can't bring them back but I conjure
How they might be if they continued.

6

Cut flowers, placed around stones with names,
Wilt in the sun, but never lose their charm.
They lose their sweet scent and bees avoid

Them and seek out living gardens, not this
Mausoleum for the campus dead whose lives
Were theirs and now we live for them instead.

Nothing spectacular, not shaped by routine.
My children must know as little about this
As possible without blinding them to facts

About life. I want stories to make them
Laugh, not lie in bed, unable to sleep, or stay
There during the day, afraid, because of what

They hear about my work life, whose cunning,
Mostly dull, changed to a sting, then to stunning.

7

That is the condition I'm in: blood
Poisoned by this campus slaughter,
Mind foggy with boats of thoughts

On water without a current, just afloat
No engines, nor sails, and that fog
So near that it eats my outstretched hand.

I step over the side and walk on this water.
Fog thick as the element that churns it up
Makes it hard to breathe and lift my legs.

This sea is littered with these boats of mine.
I keep launching them and they get stuck
And I strike out on foot and get stuck as well.

Since mid-April, bodies circle me, in my head,
With me absent from myself, as if dead.

8

I swap those dead for my desk, for my bed, for my
Children, for my office, for my dog, for my car,
For sunlight in my eyes on my morning run,

For sweat bugs chasing me on the jogging trail,
For one look from my child with love all over
That look, for one shining, weightless line

Fished at my desk from the deep blue yonder
Where my fishing line hangs without bait,
For one bite that makes sense of everything,

For I am a man on the edge of a calamity,
Stuck there after the world has moved on,
For I keep the company of dead children,

We talk about spilled blood and dead flesh,
How to live good and keep thoughts fresh.

Part Thirteen

1

Once, long ago, in a place hardly
Pinpointed on Peters' or Mercator's
Projections, a pregnant woman

Poked a caiman with a stick and it
Charged at her and she ran so fast
She mowed through a hedge and left

Her shape there. That woman was
My mother and she carried me.
That caiman chases me in my sleep.

As if it swallowed a clock stuck
At that very hour back in that time
And everywhere I go no matter what

I do brings back that caiman's shape,
With its sprint on all fours, mouth agape.

2

Twice, more recent, I met a man
In my office for some creative talk.
Dali drew that map with an egg mix

For paint and the compass was string
Held over a burning candle and wax
Fell on me like I was caught miles

From shelter in a tropical down
Pour, one that chokes gutters and leaves
You ankle deep and mindful of sagging

Powerlines, the kind you praise at 6am
For wearing modest lace flown from the East
Beaded with jewellery made through the night.

Twice was more than enough though then
I thought nothing of it and forgot about him.

3

That caiman was an iguana and your mother
Carried your brother not you. She was eighteen.
She left for England where you came along

Eleven months after your brother so that you
Two grew up like twins though he looked
Twice your size since she was anaemic

And did not know it when she fell with you.
Hence the shock of red hair on your head
That made an old English woman say

To your mother that red hair and brown skin
Made you a freak of nature. Your mother
Never replied to that woman's insult.

It left her speechless, and by retelling her
Tale, she fashions a riposte. My red hair

4

Meant something, what I do not know.
It saved me from anonymity, or marked
Me for insult. Everything became an omen

In that Caribbean of my making and so
When a man strolls into my sphere
And makes the kind of history that leaves

Us in the lower echelons of Dante's hell,
Or the nether reaches of evolution,
First, I put it down to chance then I think,

Trust how when science runs out of sums,
In waltzes robed and beaded dancers,
With shac-shac beans in hefty gourds,

Ululating to keep things as they are,
So the fabric does not deteriorate further.

What happens next always happens in real
Life, I wrote earlier. When I meant to say, I wish
No such reality on anyone, on a road already

Replete with potholes, bandits and traffic,
Coming at you in your lane, because that
Stretch of road's the only part that won't shatter

Axles or break wheels clean off. One such wheel over
Took me on Highway 101, just a wheel
Travelling above the limit of 55mph.

Traffic parted and braked for it until it failed
To make one bend too many in life, skidded along
A barrier, and careened to extinction down a steep

Embankment; laid to rest among daisies,
Our unfortunate wheel looked like it had always

6

Been there. I never saw the remainder
Of the car that wheel belonged to, but looked
Left and right for the rest of my drive

Home, where I sounded as matter-of-fact
As possible, when I relayed the tale of said
Wheel on Highway 101. This is America,

Not Ghana or Guyana. A man walks on fire,
Eats broken glass, and swallows swords
For a living. His wife sticks foot-long needles

Through her mouth and arms and sides.
Their children's bodies turn pretzel shapes
For tourists ready to buy a few snapshots

For the album back home, where the family
Stares and wonders if this is trick photography.

7

No tricks involved in this hustle,
This breakdance with the everyday.
Ordinary things drug my eyes to sleep:

A hummingbird flicks across the yard,
Stickles an arms-length from my face,
As if about to drink nectar from my eyes,

With a curved needle, changes its mind
About me, and darts into the ash trees
Leaving a sound of propellers, displaced

Air, and me stuck on the spot, in two
Minds about what to do next and doing
Nothing in the time available to me.

There is a trick to this game after all;
Not to stand too long on the spot in a lull.

8

The same can be said for grief, its nectar
Keeps me in a cave that husbands darkness.
I bump into furniture I do not recognise.

I sleep light on what feels comfortable,
Bearable, an enforced sleep, after nerves
Lose all their elasticity for numbness.

And in this house dug out of a hillside
I feel lost and at home and lose all sense
Of time and why I keep this condition.

Nectar from a flower that never runs out.
Flower that never goes out of season,
Keeping its bloom at the darkest hour,

Let me walk from that cave and off that ridge,
Fly away from that hill far from umbrage.

9

No such luck, sonny. This round-the-clock,
Mop-up phase of the operation must go on.
We'd prefer you on board rather than not.

You know the old saying, those not with us…
Say what you like, write what you want.
We pull no punches and manipulate no strings

Behind the scenes. This remains an open country.
We take pride in the right to free expression.
But we need to grab an image of your hard-drive

To prepare our case and be on the safe side.
From what you tell us you have nothing to hide,
And remember, we are on the same side.

We stand by you now as you once stood
For us when you acted in our name for our good.

10

Thanks a million (cowries). I am in your debt
For life (what's left of it). There is a benefit
When I take my children to restaurants

And the wait-staff recognise me from a course,
And they call me Sir, and mean it, and make sure
My kids know their daddy taught them and I was

Their favorite Prof, they enjoyed the talk
More than the work – and at such moments
I stop listening and study the maps of my children

For a frown or raised eyebrow and chart this:
You paid them to say that didn't you?
I did not. I would not. I could not afford it.

Few things in this journey come unheralded:
Unsolicited praise; a gunman's rampage.

11

I wear a black mask on a blue face.
I surprise myself when I think, high tech
Lynching may be invoked, if it helps

My case, if it makes them throw up their hands
At this historical moment. I'll only go there if
They fail to strike me from their list of fall guys.

That's how unstrung the instrument of my
Nerves appears at this time when a front door
Asks that I approach it with caution, sideways

Never to throw it open to someone I do not know,
So that my door becomes a foxhole with me peeking
Out before I test the front lawn with my bare feet.

My home turned to my prison, never.
A dead man's influence from the grave. Clever.

Part Fourteen

1

Say it loud, I'm black and tenured,
Pa-da, da-da, dah, dah.
Times change but the beat remains

As back dislocating as ever
As hip is to hop is to scotch is to kick
Seed on the good foot on a diorama

Etched in dirt with stone or stick,
Chalk if lucky, on concrete if blessed.
Do you believe? In love? In life

After death? In ghosts? I believe
Now means something to me
As then meant something to those

Who fell to the sound of firecrackers
Captured on a cell and several cochleas.

2

Charge me with theft of power
But I plugged my laptop into a wall
Belonging to the Port Authority

As I surfed for free at the airport
By the stone-grey and buckled sea
On my way to sundry papers

Delivered by hand and passed from eye
To mouth to ear in measured feet.
The fun part, food and drink and music,

And the funny part, a bunch of academics
Trying to dance but looking as if
Struck by electric prods intermittently,

Programmed to enjoy themselves
At the allotted hour, pardoned from bookshelves.

3

One threw his body against his class
Door and held it shut as his students crawled
Out windows. A student paused with one foot

Out and one foot in the room pondering
Whether to hang back and help out,
But the good Prof waved him off and that

Should not be the last thing heard
From the old man who survived
Auschwitz to come to this, but he kept his body

Braced there until he caught bullets
Fired through that door, all this, here,
In small-town Blacksburg, Virginia,

Of all places, where Our Daily Bread
Smells so unlike those ovens full of Nazi dead.

4

I meet her weekly at her sub-station, licking stamps
For my envelopes and making small talk
With the ferocity of a small town aficionado.

She took his parcel a little after 9am
Where he detoured between hits,
She corrected the postcode for NBC

And may or may not have said what she
Always said to me, Can I help you with
Anything else? And knowing him a little

He may have shaken his head rather than
Spared her a, no thanks, or perhaps that day
He managed to do both as last courtesies.

She says she cannot stop thinking about
Their exchange, that left its bitter in her mouth.

5

Don't take it on, I tell her, how could you know.
You help us all when we fumble coins,
Forget stamps and write or omit details

You kindly remind us about. You ferry
Our mail across land, air and sea.
And maybe we could entrust our souls

With you for that last journey from this
Land to that other place where souls go
To get weighed and parcelled off to purgatory.

If anyone should take my soul on a boat
Let it be your weight behind the oar
And you poised at the back for ballast.

Then my soul would steady its trembling;
Then I would be still and accept my fate.

6

Like the perpetual stamps that you tried
To sell me when I complained about the
Hike in the price of a first class stamp.

They came in books of twenty, you said,
And I declined to buy my way into perpetuity.
Fool that I was not to know a good thing

When I see it. Instead I purchased a few
Make up stamps to use the ones I already
Owned at the old price, and felt compelled

To get rid of no matter what the new deal.
You asked me again if I was sure since they
Might run out and... no thanks, I interrupted.

That's me, set in my ways come rain or shine,
Making my bed of nails and lying in it for all time.

Part Fifteen

1

You cross-gendered conundrum,
Painted nails and lips, baldpate,
Breasts and a kind word for all,

Your Adam's apple is a dead give-
Away, but who cares if our mail
Arrives in good time, in one piece.

This town with one of everything,
Needs you more than you need it.
You should be on the town poster,

Your face as big as a billboard
For strangers to know whether
They should keep going or stop

For food, fuel and a bed for the night;
Our Stonewall, Bus Boycott and lamplight.

2

Today I am more black than white.
Yesterday I felt no allegiance to either
Race and wanted to be human pure and

Simple, free of infractions and history,
Nursing old wounds some of whose scars
I run my mind over on my body politic.

A half-day in the sun brings out the Negro
In me and my children hardly seem to know
Who I am, when I walk in on their oval table

Talk, about my youngest son teased by a class
Mate for being a 'brown boy'. The portion
That really gets to me is the boy part.

I tell my son to remind the child what his name is,
And only call him 'pink boy' back, if he persists.

3

Of course I asked him to tell his teacher first.
In fact we followed up with a class visit to make
Sure the teacher was in on this and she seemed

Suitably appalled and promised to snuff out that
Particular fire before it gathered wind, and so on,
Until there comes a day when a rainbow in the sky

Does not bring a squint or flutter to the naked eye,
When a little black boy and a little white girl and so
Forth, until that time do not lacerate my children

With tongues of fire and expect me to sit back,
Arms folded. I will respond as I see fit since my
Son has yet to grow the necessary armour to get

Through a life in a day of this nation, as it slouches
Towards Jerusalem to avoid being still born.

4

Oh unbecoming nation. Your best moment and worst
Might be that frontier that you faced with a Smith
And Wesson over your shoulder and a holster

Stuffed with a revolver and bullets for a belt.
Was the dark bearable then? And if it was not,
You emptied your clips into it and howled.

The days measured out in sand dunes, crossed
On horseback, and rivers tacked for the shallowest
Part to wade to the other side, where you walked

Until the wind and sun dried clothes on your back.
Where another mountain range stared you down.
And another river drew a line in the dirt and dared

You to step over it and you cocked your guns
And took that step into an eternity of standoffs.

Part Sixteen

1

My last tango in Blacksburg
With my hard-drive featured orange
Juice, the colour of margarine, spilled

Working when I reached for my grub,
No sparks flew but my laptop rearranged
Its planetary glow down to the nib of a quill.

The IT guy in the department scratched
His head and dried my drive and saved
Almost all my files by removing the flatbed

Brainbox and stuffing it in a new thing-i. I have
Not said motherboard deliberately trying my best
Not to think of my discovery in '75 of Parliament:

George Clinton in bellbottoms and platforms,
Gave gravity the slip; my other Funky President.

2

George or Tapazukie and his call to arms,
MPLA, Natty going on a holiday.
I was a young eighteen and had to look up

The acronym, but the idea of a fight
As a holiday, Butlins or Disneyland, say,
Made me picture that natty dread

As war ready, armed only with his locks
That he planned to let loose with a headshake
Manufacturing lightning and thunder

In quantities that could fell an army.
If not his head, then his staff thumped,
That sends a rumble along enemy ranks.

I bring them now to my side and my aid,
To fight my dread and spread of its plague.

3

Two handguns and more than enough ammo.
All quiet as he pauses to reload and restart.
His methodical walk up and down the rows.

People I talk to, people I see all the time
Around campus lying on the floor behind desks.
He aims at them and fires again and again.

My opposing army of music and dance
Sounds like the equivalent of placing flowers
In rifle barrels and chanting cross-legged.

He left me his acts and I bring all my past
To bear on what he did as a way to cope
With the fact that I, too, am left tasting sour.

I summon my army to occupy this space:
Horns, strings, voice, drum and bass.

4

Twist, shout, swing left, dip right,
Tell the DJ, don't stop unless he wants
A riot on his hands, this is serious,

This is disco, dance till you drop.
Sweat like peas, we cleared the room
Of desks and chairs and left it empty

For this wall of speakers and two turn-
Tables and strobe lights so strong
They might induce epilepsy.

There's no time to think this through,
There's a gaping wound only the vibes
Can stitch up and music close and keep

Sealed against the pictures of the fallen
Lying in postures of the grave and sullen.

Part Seventeen

1

In a decent work of fiction
There would be a twist, a turn
Right in the middle that the most astute

Reader misses or guesses wrong.
In this lyric there's no such plot
The whole story remains ever present,

Charts an ever changing feeling
For events of that Poetry Month Monday.
Imagine a trowel smoothing concrete

Adding to those layers and smoothing
A thicker and thicker wall, well, that's how
The lyric builds meaning in a deepening circle,

Except the concrete never dries
And the worker with that trowel never dies.

2

Trauma shares the same toolkit and pool
Of itinerant workers and the same well made
Thing results after hours of hard labour.

What does this mean for art, for our practice,
If that which instils pleasure also stirs up trauma?
The literary journalist asks in a headline.

It means you, Sir, have been away from your desk
Too long to know your ass from your face.
It means you are asking the wrong question.

Art imitates life in so far as during
The poem's making there is no other
Place for the artist to turn but life:

What's made stands for the living we did then,
Or might have done if we did nothing.

3

Here's the thing. I had my eyes peeled
For danger but tracked the wrong man.
The one I followed wore a long trench

Coat and wide-brimmed hat and carried
A briefcase, the kind I saw in *Day of the
Jackal*, cushioning a rifle in sections

Ready for assembly. He wrote about
Dissecting women with a surgeon's eye
For sinews which makes him a good writer.

But he talked the same line as his pen.
There was no daylight between the person
In the fiction, and the writer sitting opposite me.

I saw him walking off the page to carry out
The number of slayings he wrote about.

4

What game are we in, psychopathology
Of the everyday, or serving the muse?
A little bit of both and not much of either,

Sounds like the same sin-ting but it isn't.
That the killer stays in my head's a matter
For the people in white coats, that he persists

In my art's a matter for form to contain him
So that he does not run riot with my art,
For each task I need both sides in my corner,

Otherwise, not much gets written, and electrodes
May as well be glued to my temples, and a strong
Current swept through my skull to calm me.

That bed shared by two unlikely bedfellows,
Resembles a sky shared by sun and moon.

Part Eighteen

1

All the days of my life (not that many)
Squashed into one (that's too few)
Early mornings spent at the tobacco

Confectionary Mr Hill ran as a corner
Shop where I delivered newspapers,
And parted company fast with my pocket

Money earned from that paper round,
Including a ten-speed bike bought
From a catalogue and paid for in weekly

Instalments and parked in the shed
Not twenty yards from our front door,
That some hoodlum broke into and stole,

That Mr Hill at 3am armed with a crowbar
Failed to find in numberless sheds cranked open.

2

Blackheath Hill in South London
Crisscrossed from 5.30am to 7.00am
Stuffing dailies into front-door boxes

Avoiding yard dogs tearing those head
Lines and one morning a woman in nothing
But red hair who must have been near birth

Pulling open her door to tell her departed
Husband something important and coming
Face-to-face with me: for the longest moment

We looked each other up and down before
She slammed her door in my face and I stuffed her
Paper in her letter box and beat a hasty retreat.

Her and the odd sight of a fox-sprint
Across the hill, and me covered in newsprint.

3

By the time I was ready for school I was
Ready for bed but I knocked back cereal,
Toast and tea, grabbed my books and ran

To the bus stop and queued with the workers
Who looked at me as if to say, *make the most*
Of those books sonny or end up like us

Wishing we'd paid attention in class to those
Books and that teacher to avoid this
Drudgery for a pay packet that stretches so far

And no farther and overtime that eats up
All the free space in my head, all the free
Time I dreamed about and the things in it.

All that in one look and nothing said
By the lips of the living, working, dead.

4

All this recollection for the lives curtailed,
As if they'd lived theirs, a little this way,
With a past taken care of and a future

Based on that past, and their fingerprint
On the present with a pet to exercise
Come morning and friends to meet at dusk,

And no inkling that any of this could come
To an end in the way it did for them
In the middle of getting on with their day,

Ending all of the search through the bits
And pieces of a life for the rust and the gems,
And the things that need a little dusting

To be right as rain you can safely drink,
Safer than the water that falls into your sink.

5

Why bring up Mr Hill now I don't rightly
Know, he jumped into the front of my head
From the murky deep at the back and stayed

Shining for such a long time I had to do
Something about him. There's no link
Between them and him, except for me,

And there's no way this generation of iPods
Would ever do what I did for extra money,
But those actions amount to a past

And remembering them amounts to a life,
And maybe I see their deaths as robbery
Of this simple gift of reflection and for them

I look back and I come up with alternatives
To the frozen brain and dried blood in veins.

6

Making weekly payments for that bike
After it was pinched proved the hardest thing.
I worked for something missing and I looked

Long and hard at every cycle that passed me
Thinking mine might turn up by chance.
It never materialised in all that time of paying

The catalogue and I always approached that
Door, with the pregnant woman, in a hurry
To get away, secretly hoping to meet her

Again in her finery without knowing what
I'd do if she opened her door just for me,
Just as I geared-up to stick the paper in.

But that's how I worked with surprises,
And that's how surprise works on me.

Part Nineteen

1

Thunder shook the element that heated
My coffee cup in my first-floor home-office.
Rain rioted against the windows.

I answered the phone just as my love
Stepped out of the shower and she called
Me in a rather soft voice for her call.

I signalled that I was on the phone
And she stood in my office door
Moments later holding up a Post-It

Note that said, action, in cursive.
I cut short that phone call and caught
Up with her in the master bedroom.

Thunder kept us close, a warm rain
Glistened on our pasted bodies.

2

The world is not right for another
Child to be brought into it but we
Were not making more children.

The thought came from thinking about
Dead babies, the babies our children
Remain to us throughout their lives.

If you bury a child the rest of your life
Spoils even though you live it as best
As you can and never let on to others.

When I touched you in a loving way
I fought off pictures of our children
Dead before their time, dead before us:

When we hugged I left no room for air
Other than hers exhaled into my face.

3

I want our children so safe I'd
Rewind the clock until they were unmade
And separated in our separate bodies;

Yours and mine. Each of us
Would be the guardian of our children
In as complete a fashion as humanly

Possible given the parameters of flesh.
Sending them off to college would prove
An interesting affair, having them leave

Home and find that neither parent
Was left there in that proverbial empty
Nest and when our children fall in love

We act as chaperones in the most complete
Sense of the term blocking all indiscretion.

4

We don't let them develop; they remain
With puppy fat and hair on them so soft
We called it bumfluff; we won't let them eat

More than us and we pick at our food
At our advanced age; we won't allow them
Dreams other than the ones we harbour.

We do all this to safeguard against death
By motorcycle, death my falling off a mountain,
Death by failed parachute, death by partying

With such vigour the house comes crashing
Down; death by skis; death by drowning
In a hail of bullets in the middle of a class:

We welcome death to our octogenarian bed;
Happy all our children stayed safe in our head.

Part Twenty

1

If 1000mph were a way in the world
I'd have my way with Doris
By now instead of this body count.
If hollow point were Jefferson Forest
And not a condition for rancour,
I'd want to catch one myself, get
Two or three or four.

But speed, barrel and hollow point
Work in unison for one end, girl,
Several ends and I'm near yet
Not so close that I matter,
Not far away enough to ignore the trigger
Squeezed by a hand I took in greeting,
A touch that's a touch all the same however fleeting.

2

A fleet of ambulances not one in a hurry
An emergency of scale not scope
If cloud were laundry in a tub
Then two strong arms took two
Ends and wrung them out over this town
Causing a downpour in a sky full of eyes

Eyes as red as if rubbed in cayenne or curry
An urgency plaited into a long rope
In a hey ho and a rub a dub dub
So very much pleased to meet you
Even if said mouth sideways by a clown
Even with eyes with many red eyes for a sky

All this as I knelt and played and scrubbed
My getaway alloy wheels' chrome hubs

Part Twenty-One

1

Blood under ultraviolet light
Waits for a cold case enthusiast,
Blood mashed into grainy wood,

Scraped by speckle and mounted
Under a microscope, brings them
Back to life, in our talk, at some time

When the future is ready to be invented
As truth, sought and found and accepted,
Rather than the kind designed around

Nods, handshakes and the Class of '69
Whoever they may be in whatever
Size, shape or form or manifestation.

The dead want nothing, how can they
Want anything, the living need them.

2

The dead cannot sing with dust
In their windpipes and the ampoules
Of lungs dried as bagpipes in a museum.

The dead cannot speak from the grave
Contrary to paranormal pyrotechnics
In grainy-lit footage of Big Foot sightings

And ghostly stirrings in antiquated attics.
The dead eat what worms take from them;
Worms cut tunnels in the flats of the dead.

The dead digest memories of themselves
Made in the world of the living without
Knowing what exactly they have eaten.

They take what they get from the living
They wear makeup applied by the living.

3

A dead man can be found at the bottom
Of a rum bottle, a dead woman can be
Found in the leaves of a drained teapot.

Both wish to be read like a book; both
Speak to us as we sound in our heads,
And they appear as we knew them

Before death took them from us,
They look younger and in their Sunday
Best and they come with instructions

For the living, something we need to hear,
Obvious, that needed saying, before it means
Anything to our plans and our actions.

We dream how they died that they may live;
Our dreams refresh our memories of them.

4

The student I knew appears as a queen
Of basketball leading a franchise to victory.
She dunks the basketball with her left hand

While waving to me in the audience
With her right. She tells me poetry works
Best if left to its own devices and I believe

Her without question, not for what she said,
But how she makes it sound like some
Thing that was there waiting to be said.

Something that once said cannot be denied.
And though she was young she looked even
Younger in a baggy uniform and trainers;

Much like a girl on the verge of becoming
A woman or a woman still two parts the girl.

5

One year later finds me like back then,
Shaking my head as if a repeated gesture
Changes the facts or shakes them off
My body where they hook themselves,
Thirty-three fishhooks, one hook for
Each name, buried in me, one hook
For each life lost. Each person caught
Me on a lifeline, took one look at me
Then threw me back for another one
To catch me, hardly a glance and cut
That line and fling me again into that
Element each must fish me from
As they exit from this world, hooks
With their names sunk in my flesh.

6

Were the big 'A', little,
no bigger, no less testy,
than the aperture of the needle
my grandmother made me thread
with a lick of frayed cotton, one
eye, my weaker left, closed,
for her to stitch the button
onto the shirt on my back
after a pinch in lieu of any
mishap dished out by a slip
by that needle in her unsteady
thimble-on-middle-finger hand;

7

were the six of sixteen
a hook held in April waters
all month for the one big bite
and my pull against its tug
with the sweet in sixteen
extracted from the number's
molasses by sucking on a pinhole
in the apex of a mottled egg,
I'd be left with bitters –
the Brook lax we ate
thinking it was chocolate,
the Senna pod leaves we knocked

8

back taking it for sweet tea,
when both were laxatives;
then and only then I'd face
April 16th not as cruellest,
but as the *th* in sixteenth
now the nth degree for me
in a year of Aprils, of thirty-two,
no, thirty-three, forced to stream
through that needle's eye
whose pinch, more a stab,
takes my skin for fabric,
my eyes for buttonholes.

9

Moon with a crow at its neck
Ready to cut the artery with a claw
Spill red on front lawns
Until that moon blackens

Watch how a full head of hair
Thins in this light that strips
Things layer by layer down
To the bone and then marrow

Apply pressure to that cut
Collect that hair in a ball
Before that crow carries it
Away to a nest out of reach

On a moonbeam painted red
On lawns planted with the dead

10

Index finger flicked against middle finger and thumb
Not the sound of a gun

Suck teeth, headshake, cipher circle, dozens run
Not the sound of a gun

Handclap, backslap, stilettos rap on ground
Not the sound of a gun

Knuckle crack, July 4th fireworks by the ton
Not the sound of a gun

Appalachia tut-tut, Khoisa click of the tongue
Not the sound of a gun

Drumsticks, engine backfire, pneumatic drill drum
Not the sound of a gun

I eat the spoor of the dead
When I breathe, when I walk, when I run.
They rise from underground and stay airborne.
Some lodge in the corners of my eyes and form crusts.
Others line the corners of my mouth and the lines turn
Down giving me a sour look, a frown or complaint.
Those spoors form chigoes between my toes,
Fingers and work their way to my crotch,
Until more of me is dead than living.
I am done, I am done, I am done.

Continental Shelf

Well

Plaited light muscles
Aside shadows skulking
Inside a tin bucket

Magnet for eyes
Cast of a mind
Poured and left to set

Something Giacometti
Peeled and peeled
All twisted rope

Dream parchment
If seen as a mouth
Open and about to slake

Our bodies robbed
Of flesh and bones
Skin for a gourd

Martial Art

Plants two bare feet
Three-feet apart
Knees slightly bent

One hand held away
From the body seems
About to pick fruit

Chest high the way
The fingers spread
Curl and linger

The other hand
Waits its turn
Tucked at the waist

The head faces
That fruit tree
But the eyes

Widen to swallow
All they can take in
Blind spots as well

If you watched
The hand about
To pick fruit

You missed the one
Tucked at the waist
Just as you would

Miss a rattler's
Strike if all you
Saw was what you

Heard and could do
Nothing but see

3am

Full moon parked in my back
yard, one headlamp working over
time, pooled here right now,
brazing grass, vines and stone
posed as coral and seaweed.
The child in me runs outdoors
barefoot, bareheaded and bare
arsed for a moon shower,
unlike any other until this,
till the next time I dream about
Airy Hall, Guyana and the tree
Perseverance boasts which divides
Government Road, parting
bitumen, as a comb parts
smack in the middle of my scalp
separating my head into two:
bivalves of thought and play.

So I wake forty years later
under this polished moon
seen with the same eyes
asking for more and viewing
my life spread out on the lawn
on a tablecloth made of moon
light and set with the things,
everything, from my past:
one shell pond, one field
where we kept a caiman
for a day, the coconut grove
for counting coconuts sent
down, light striated
through coconut branches,
the backdam and railway line,
then ricefields ankle deep
in trench water and a tsetse
fly balanced on a paling
fence, and so they come
unbidden in a world without
end, with beginnings I find
daily without trying to find any
thing besides this moon
which came looking and found
me in Blacksburg, Virginia.

Jump Rope

We skipped rope we three did,
Skipped for the hell of it, no dare,
No doh ray me, nor stick and carrot.
For the jump, the landing and wait
One fraction, just a tick, weight poised
On the balls of feet, the intake of perfume
Into the perforated air intake, three kids
Free to exhale, air not ours, air
We borrowed to holler a name not
Ours, but written daily on our slate
Or else, a name that fetched what noise
We made and owned all headroom.

There to be hoorayed if a name
Could be fruit, ripe and at play
On the lowest branch, not chipped
By bird, reptile or beast. So
We hopped and dropped, our kind
In a bouncing, flouncing, trouncing game.
Three buds guided by the same
Torchlight, our lives led astray,
Astride a border of rope, we skipped.
Up, down, up, down, up, and no
Down for the frame of mind
We were in, hemmed in by that frame.

Us framed, three, in a mind to be one.
Three, and a piece of string for a border.
How long I cannot tell now, removed
Now from that day to this till kingdom
Becomes republic, gone too those two,
And that border guarded by that beast.
The border dispute turned our rope burn
Into a rope trick. Those hops, in air drier
Than usual, that name, not our groove,
Played on lips free to call it to come
Out of hiding. Minds open for true
For the first time and last but not least.

Moonwalk

1

Polish made moon so bright
A cloth woven with cloud
Dragged from side to side by
Wind whipped up by a tide
Sun slapped on liberally
Static from that rub
Down spawned lightning
Thunder sent to the four corners
Compasses keep at the bottom
Of seas where that deep shine
From that moon shoe rap tap
Tapping its illuminated path
From end to end in a vast sky
Falls into fabric that consumes
Every last scrap of its shine
For something likened to dying
Under a heavy blanket with no
Energy to brush it aside and no
Reason to do anything more
Than keep still and hold breath

2

I saw this very moon in a yard
Ringed with a paling fence
Why that moon filled a pool
For children to play bat and ball
Stopped only by one shadow
Cast as a house sailing across
That yard to block our sight

Time knows since all I know
Is the flavour of that moon
Back then summoned some
Thing I try to keep close
As one keeps a pillow by
The head and as a mouth
Keeps counsel with its tongue

Star Fruit

for Liliana

Sonar detects my brittle Pleiades
All skull and bundled crossbones
Adrift in quantum womb-gunk.
I cut you from your moorings,
Wash grease from blue skin
Oxygen turns medium-rare.

Your eight pounds, fifteen ounces
Fit between my elbow and wrist.
Butterfly breaths, tadpole heartbeats,
Subwoofer, wah-wah amplifier
Quieted by current from two poised
Nipples in a silent movie of sustenance.

Baby, I could gobble you up,
Call me Cannibal, for you
Seasoned with love, I cradle
You just as I once held
The honeyed hearts from young
Coconut trees, uprooted, cracked

Open, supped on and marvelled at,
By us barefoot, raggedy children
In Airy Hall, Guyana; what
Unguarded flesh beginnings
For thirty-foot plus coconuts,
So high we called them star fruit.

Continental Shelf

Guyana climbed from my colonised bed,
Blindly stuffed feet into my leather slippers

And ambled towards kitchen and coffee
Where the dog wagged to be let out

On the lawn and Monday morning rushed,
Uninvited, in my garlanded front door.

Guyana reached for the corners of my robe
Wrapped around contours accustomed

To flags thrown over its territory.
The dog rushed back into the house

From last night's powdery snow
As the coffee pot choked on its perfume.

The refrigerator mimicked
A car idling at red lights. This country

Needs to wake up faster, for my body
Could use another couple hours rest.

Give me back my slippers, my robe
And my favourite cup purchased at Whately

Diner from another life and laced with two
Per cent milk and beans from Central

America. Sit, dog, your windscreen
Wiper tail makes my eyes turn.